Dear Fellow Teacher,

The purpose of this guide is to provide a comprehensive, [...] book. For years, I have dragged around photocopying sheets that [...] textbooks (occasionally opened), and hundreds of random activity [...] I had also spent a lot of money on numerous supply teaching books for Lower and Upper Primary, but the majority of the activities required photocopying. Photocopying codes are rarely given out and even if you do get access to one, they are often occupied, difficult to use or you don't have enough time. I used to print some on my own time and dime, costing me a fortune in ink, or I was spending nearly $10 a day to have 3 activity sheets for the class, ready to go for 'just in case.'

When the teacher had left a plan, activities would often go shorter than expected, Internet logins wouldn't work, resources weren't available and the class was doing everything they could so that you could not teach the History lesson prescribed. Things go wrong, and the biggest asset to a supply teacher is to be prepared for the unexpected and to be good at thinking on your feet. This book will give you the ability to cope in most situations, from having no planning provided, to fun time-fillers guaranteed to engage all ages. You will also find all the tips and organisational tools you will need to be a successful supply teacher.

....

This guide is set into 10 different sections.

Tips	Organiser	Daily Plan and Notes	Literacy	Numeracy

Art	Drama and Music		Games	PE / Outdoor Games

Each section is broken up into activities that are suited to either **LOWER PRIMARY** (4 - 8 years), or **UPPER PRIMARY** (8 - 12 years) or both.

All the activities need little to no resources and the resources needed are underlined in the activity. The pack also includes templates and items that may be useful.

Resources included:

- Daily Plan Template
- School Year Calendar
- Daily Plan suggestions and outline

- Professional Development recording sheet
- Financial Records sheet
- Activities for all Primary levels

I hope this makes your days easier and successful, giving you return calls and plenty of work.

Enjoy!

Kelly

TEACHER FOR A DAY

Getting Started, Engaging Students and Succeeding as a Supply, Relief or Substitute Teacher

Primary School Edition
Second Edition

by Kelly Quilter

Illustrations by
Emmanuel Sambayan

For my kids,

Van and Neve

the reason I have to go to work.

TABLE OF CONTENTS

CONTENTS

Games

PE / Outdoor Games

Everyone is a genius. But if you judge a fish by its ability to climb a tree, it will live its whole life believing that it is stupid.

-Albert Einstein

Register. Go online and register with your state's governing bodies for Supply Teachers. Also register your details on sites such as Emergency Teachers Australia or Class Cover. Don't forget to contact Public, Private and Catholic sectors to increase your chances of employment.

Go door knocking. Take your resume to any school that you can get yourself to. Some may only take online resumes, while others may get filed in the bin but it could still work in your favour by being in the right place at the right time. I know people who have gained their own class for the year simply by doing this.

Timing. Go to schools as soon as you graduate, before the school year, around Day 8 and through the flu season, as these are the times many schools are looking for staff.

Volunteer. One day of volunteering might be all it takes. Offer to help with reading groups, special needs, anywhere that you can be of assistance.

Network. Use all the contacts you have. Anyone that is a teacher, teacher aide, groundsman or cleaner might be able to give you a good word and an in to a day's supply. The rest is up to you.

Teaching Practicum. Work hard and leave a good impression and the door will always be open for future work. You already know how the school works so you are an easy choice when it comes to hiring supply staff.

Be professional. When visiting a school in any capacity ensure that you are always professional in your attire and your manner. You will gain more respect if you look and act the part.

Smile. Be friendly, approachable and pleasant. Say hi or smile to other staff, make them think you are one of them, and hopefully you will be soon enough. A smile can go a long way.

Think outside the box. Try something different. Schmooze the office ladies when you hand in your resume with a box of chocolates. Send the HR or Principal a digital portfolio demonstrating your skills. Use your nephew, niece or neighbour to drop off at school and swing by the office with them.

14 Tips To Make Your Day Run Smoother

1. Arrive early to orientate yourself with the school, classroom and daily plan. Ensure you know the school's behaviour management system and their break times.

2. Be prepared to teach any grade or specialist classes. You may get booked teaching Year 2 only to find you are teaching Music when you get there.

3. Check if you have Eating Duty as well as a Playground Duty. Make sure you know where the duty areas, folders, vests and first aid kits are located.

4. Find out whether the class has specialist lessons and if you have to drop them off or pick them up. If you do, ask where you will need to go for the Non-Contact Time.

5. Often a plan will be left for you. If not ask a neighbouring teacher for any ideas on what the students have been learning. This not only helps you to keep the kids in a familiar routine, it also gets you acquainted with other teachers.

6. Look through some students' desks to see if they have any workbooks you can work directly from e.g., Maths, English, Handwriting. Also look at their previous work to see what level they are working at.

7. After calling the roll, get students to tell you their names again and maybe say one thing about themselves. It can really help your day if you can learn at least a few names.

8. For younger students, get them to tell you their class rules and behaviour management system. For all students, reiterate that just because there's a different teacher and you might do some things differently, it doesn't mean the rules change.

9. Gauge early on (or ask other teachers) whether it is a challenging class and implement some other behaviour management techniques. Refer to Page 17 for ideas.

10. If there is a plan, try your best to stick to it and mark the work you feel confident to mark by the end of the day.

11. Try to do whole class activities unless it is a routine group activity. It will help keep the class in order.

12. Introduce yourself to administration staff and teachers and go to the staffroom at break if you can. The more familiar other staff are with you the more likely they will request you for work.

13. Make sure you have a hat, whistle and appropriate shoes for all terrain. You never know what lunch duty you might be put on.

14. Leave a tidy classroom and a note for the teacher at the end of the day stating the work you have covered and marked, class behaviour and any issues.

BEHAVIOUR MANAGEMENT TIPS

• Set the tone from the start. Make sure students are lining up quietly before entering the class or that they are sitting quietly at their desks.

• Remember, some classes will try to take advantage of your temporary role in their class, but try to be confident and assertive at all times. The class will never be as well-behaved for you as their own teacher, so pick your battles and bribe them!

• That said, be firm and consistent with your expectations and follow the class or school's behaviour plans as best you can.

• Try not to resort to yelling. A calm, quiet voice or a stern look can be just as effective in a chaotic classroom.

• If a lesson isn't working, don't keep persevering with it. Stop and move to a new activity but ensure that they think it is your idea and not because of the disruptions. Choose an activity you know will engage them, even if it diverts from the teacher's plan. Control of the classroom is key if you are going to get through the day.

• If the classroom teacher lets certain students on the computer, sit on a cushion, fiddle with a squishy ball, etc., don't fight it. Check with a responsible student what the norm is and don't let them take advantage, but don't try to change their ways if it will cause more upheaval than it is worth. Remember, you are only there short term.

• Send challenging students on special jobs with someone responsible to distract or diffuse any potential issues.

• Take a difficult student aside and speak to them one on one away from the class. This way they cannot get the attention from peers that they usually crave. Explain that you don't want to embarrass them in front of the class and ask them if they have any problems they would like to discuss with you. Explain that you are unhappy with their behaviour and suggest that they change it now or there will be further consequences.

• If any behaviour gets out of hand or dangerous to you or other students, call the Office or Behaviour Teacher immediately. Be sure to write down the incident so the teacher can formally record it.

• Use stickers or a stamp to reward positive behaviour. Students of all ages love receiving even the smallest recognition for their work.

• Use lots of positive praise, particularly for the younger students. Be careful not to give older students too much obvious praise, as it can seem 'uncool' amongst peers. An acknowledging nod or thumbs up might be better received for the older grades.

• Find a time filler/game that the class likes and use it to get students to work well throughout the day for the chance to play it more.

• Use a hacky sack or a ball to get students to read aloud or answer questions in the class to get them more involved and engaged. Very useful for older students.

BEHAVIOUR MANAGEMENT STRATEGIES

Outline your expectations for their behaviour and what the disciplinary actions will be.

Wait for Silence

If the class is very rowdy and you are finding it hard to gain control, stand up front in silence. Write on the board Time in at Lunch and write tally marks or numbers until the class is silent. They will soon pick up on what you are doing.
Give them a chance to work off the minutes if they are working well.
Great for older students.

1, 2, 3 Rule

Verbal Warning - Address the student's behaviour first.

1st Warning - student gets their name on the board.

2nd Warning - student gets a mark on their name and they will have timeout or 5 minutes in at lunchtime.

3rd Warning - student is removed from the activity, sent to buddy room if needed or will have 10 minutes in at lunchtime.

Ticks and Crosses

Write everyone's name on the board and give them a tick for positive behaviour and a cross for poor behaviour. This helps to learn students' names too.
The people with the most ticks can have free time/prize. Three crosses means the student will have to stay in at lunchtime.

+/- Tally Time

This works as a whole class strategy. Put tally marks up on the board for time in (−) and free time (+). Each tally mark is a minute that they will either remain inside at lunchtime or gain free time or game time at the end of the day.

Bounce Detention

The first person to talk gets their name up on the board and has 1 minute in at lunchtime. The next person to talk then replaces the first name on the board and has 2 minutes in at lunch. This continues, adding on a minute until everyone stops talking. Works well for older students.

FREE TIME reward

FREE TIME is written up on the board. Explain to the class that every time the class is off task a letter will be rubbed off. The class needs to have at least one letter remaining at the end of the day to get some free time, be it a class game or their own choice of activity. You change this word to suit your reward e.g., Game time, Sport time, etc.

Prize Bag

Use a prize bag with pencils, rubbers, toys from the dollar store, etc. Hand out raffle tickets for positive behaviour that get placed in a box/container/hat. Draw out a winner at the end of the day to choose a prize. This allows even the most challenging child a chance to win. You could also tell the class you might draw more than one prize depending on how well they behave all day. Have a discussion on chance and the likelihood of winning. The prizes might cost you a little but it's a small price to pay to help you have a smooth sailing day.

Rewards Cards

Give out specially designed business cards as a unique reward for a select few children at the end of the day or during lessons.

Positive Rewards

Stickers, Stamps and Certificates are the perfect, inexpensive way to reinforce positive behaviour. It could be a sticker for the children working hard, a stamp for those showing good listening or a certificate or card for children showing kind behaviour. Giving more attention to positive behaviours will encourage them to do so more frequently.

Teacher vs Student

Draw up a T-chart with your name versus the class. You get a point every time they are talking or off task. They get a point when they are working well and making good choices. At the end of each session they can get a game as their reward if they win. If you win they must continue working. Give out points generously, especially at the start and try and ensure they are a few points ahead of you most of the time.

Appoint a Leader

Choose someone to be your class leader. This student can be your special helper for a set period (an hour, a session) as well as the Attention Grabber. You can give this student a signal, such as a thumbs up or a nod, and he or she needs to do an action (i.e., hand goes up, or a silly saying is said to the class) and the class need to copy. This is the signal for quiet and focus. Inform that you will be looking for children on their best behaviour to be the next leader.

TIPS

Saving Face

Older students will do anything to 'save face' and to ensure they look cool. Take a difficult student aside and speak to them one on one, away from the class. This way they cannot get the attention from peers that they usually crave and you can potentially avoid the situation escalating. Explain that you don't want to embarrass them in front of the class and ask them if they have any problems they would like to discuss with you.

PERMISSION TO reward

Write up some rewards on the board and tell the class that throughout the lesson a student that is working well will be allowed to choose a reward. Once the next well behaved student is chosen, their reward time (at the teacher's discretion) finishes and is handed to the next person. They can get the reward time again if they are continuously working well. Choose from the following that you think will work for you and your class.

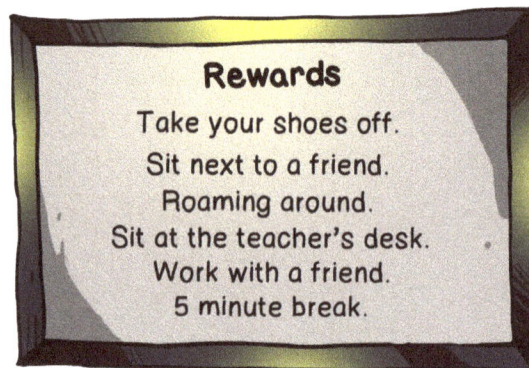

Rewards
Take your shoes off.
Sit next to a friend.
Roaming around.
Sit at the teacher's desk.
Work with a friend.
5 minute break.

Great listening

Beautiful handwriting

Thank you for your hardwork.

Post it notes

Write down positive comments and stick to students' tables as they are working.

Seating Plan

Draw up the seating plan when you get in the room then when you are calling the roll fill in their names. You can then easily refer to them by name for redirection or answering questions and will have them guessing as to how you can remember all their names so quickly!

Deli	Travis	Ande	Lilly	Sophia
Sari				Zane
Amelia				Laura
Tilly	Bonnie	Noah	Cleo	Samson
Koa				Cayden
Eva	Van	Neve	Luke	Byron

Calls to Attention

Teach the children little call and responses to get their attention. You say the first part and they answer with the second.

1, 2, 3. Eyes on me…1,2. Eyes on you.
Hands on top… Everybody stop!
Macaroni and Cheese…Yes please!
Shark bait…Hoo ha ha!
To infinity… And beyond!
Holy moly… Guacamole!
Waterfall…Shhhh!
Flat tire… Shhh!
Can I get a… Whoop! Whoop!
Stop!...Collaborate and listen!
All set?... You bet!
Ready to rock… Ready to roll!
Zip it, lock it…Put it in your pocket.

Perform a Trick

Tell them if they do fantastic listening then you will do something special for them at the end such as a cartwheel, handstand, push-ups or any other fun skill you have. They will do anything to see you being silly and you will always be fondly remembered for any wacky things you do.

Teacher Says

Teacher says "Freeze! Put your hands on your heads. Put your hands on your knees, Toes, mouth etc. until you have all the children's attention.

If you are sitting on the carpet you can do repeated patterns silently until all students catch on. Touch head, ears, head, ears. Then nose, shoulders, nose, shoulders etc.

DO'S

• Act professionally at all times.

• Move around the classroom as you teach. This lets students know your presence and looks great if other staff come in your room.

• Keep the students busy. Bored or distracted students turn into disruptive students. Get fast finishers to read a book if other activities aren't at the ready.

• Remember to pass on any notes or messages that are left for the teacher.

• Leave the room neat and tidy.

• Leave a card or note with your name so if you did a good job they can request you at a later date.

• Follow the plan as best you can.

• Leave feedback for the teacher on your day and what you covered.

• Mark work that you are confident in marking. Assessment is best left for the teacher.

• Handle behaviour situations as best as you can.

• Record any major incidents that would need to be recorded. Notify admin if necessary.

GETTING THE CALL BACK

There are certain things teachers love and hate when it comes to supply teachers. Here is a list of do's and don'ts.

• Disregard the plan unless you don't have the resources, access to tasks, etc

• Do activities in the wrong workbooks. If in doubt, use scrap paper.

• Use the teacher's personal things- cup, stickers, certificates, rewards etc.

• Leave trivial behaviour issues for the teacher to deal with the next day.

• Sit at your desk all day or use your phone in class.

• Use too much of their photocopying quota if you have been given access to it.

• Take the kids out for sport all the time. At some schools it is frowned upon for supply teachers to always do this.

BOOK SUGGESTIONS WITH ACTIVITES

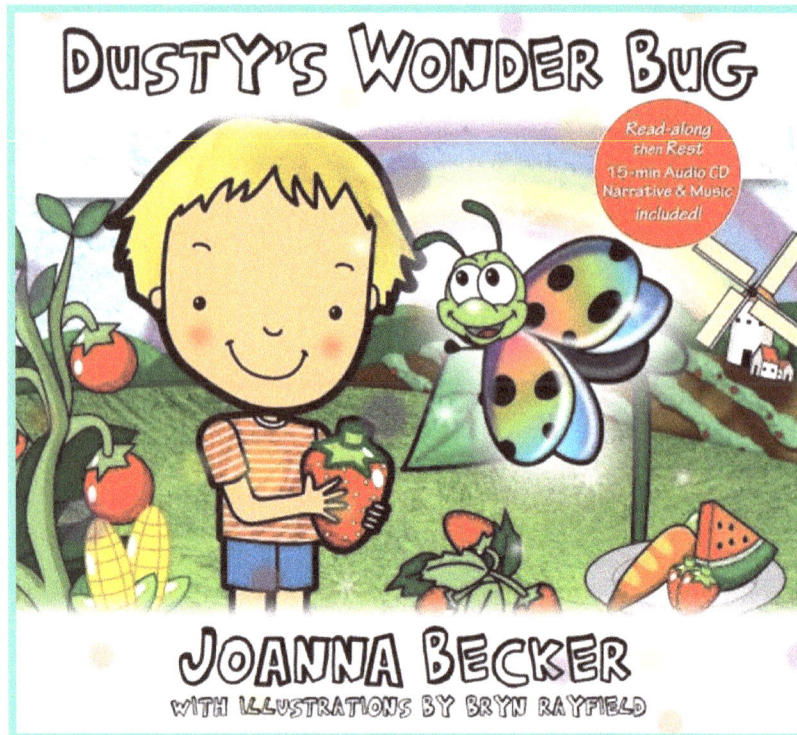

DUSTY'S WONDER BUG

Read-along then Rest 15-min Audio CD Narrative & Music included!

JOANNA BECKER
WITH ILLUSTRATIONS BY BRYN RAYFIELD

Dusty's Wonderbug by Joanna Becker (Lower Primary)

This book has endless inspiration for healthy eating and gratitude for nature.

Literacy	Numeracy	Health
Cloze activity predicting rhyming words in the book.	Count and list all the different types of fruit and vegetables in the book.	Recall and draw food that is grown in the ground and on a vine.
Retell favourite part of the story.	Sort the food into different categories e.g., colour, ground/vine/tree grown, students favourite food. Choose one, tally/count amounts then graph findings. Discuss most, least, same etc.	Write or draw your favourite food from the book. I like…
Create a new title page using yourself and a different magical creature.		Write why you believe it is important to eat healthy food and why we should be thankful.

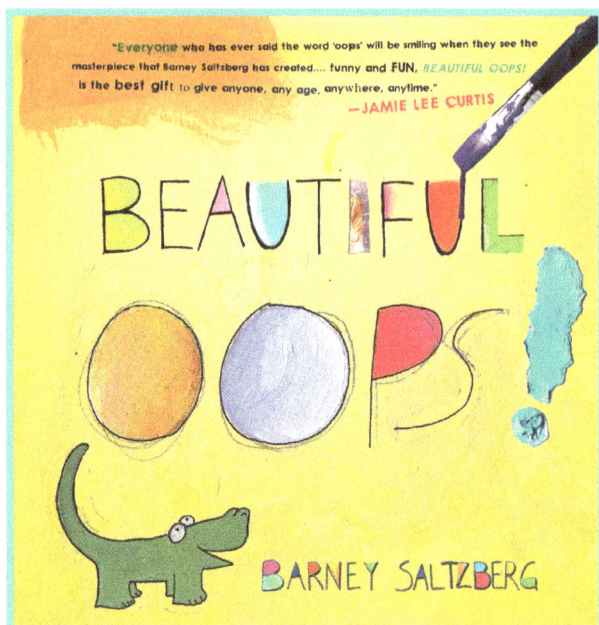

"Everyone who has ever said the word 'oops' will be smiling when they see the masterpiece that Barney Saltzberg has created.... funny and FUN, BEAUTIFUL OOPS! is the best gift to give anyone, any age, anywhere, anytime."
—JAMIE LEE CURTIS

BEAUTIFUL OOPS!

BARNEY SALTZBERG

Beautiful Oops! by Barney Salzberg (All grades)

Countless art activities using this book as inspiration. Get students to draw an 'Oops' for another student which they will then create something from it.

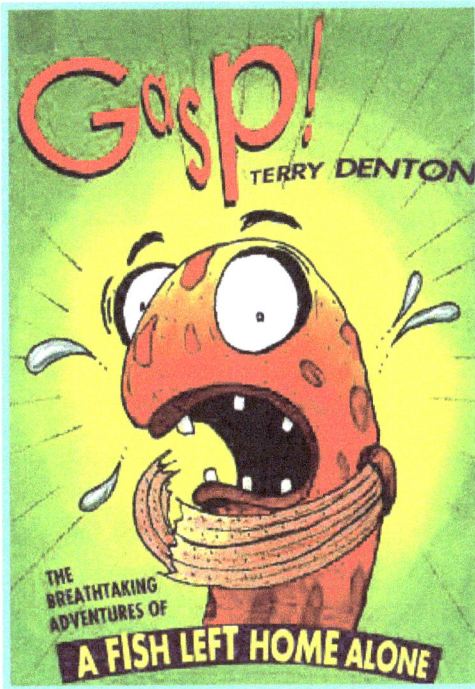

Gasp by Terry Denton (All grades)

• Read the story until page 4 (pages are numbered in reverse). Get students to predict an ending. Discuss ideas of other places the fish might find water and then get students to write their own ending using creative (bubble, wiggly, block, etc.) writing like in the book. Then get students to illustrate.

• Do a step by step illustration lesson of the fish on the front page. Simple for even Preps and non-artistic supply teachers to do.

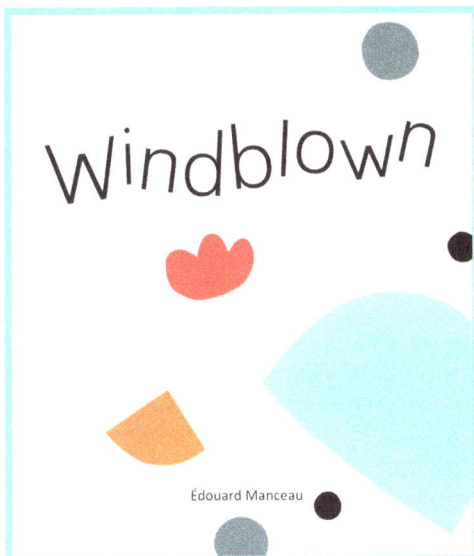

Windblown by Édouard Manceau (All grades)

A book inspired by rubbish. An art activity using a template (online or you can create your own) of the shapes used in the book; students can create their own pictures.

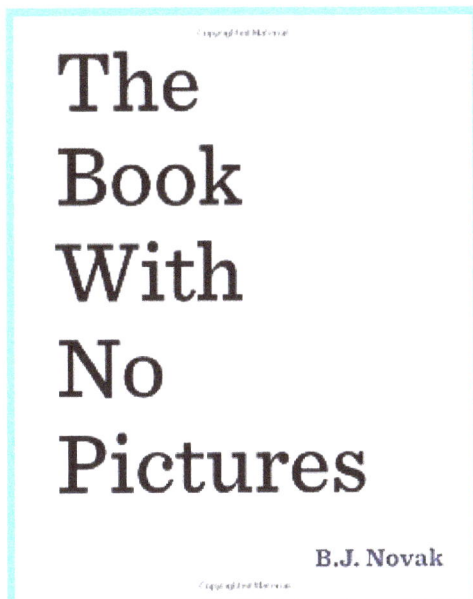

The book with no pictures by B.J Novak (All grades)

• Get students to make up their own nonsense words and define them.

• Get students to write their own page using sentence starters from the book.

• Explore noun groups.

• Get students to draw illustrations for the book.

TIPS

Mix it Up by Herve Tullet (Lower Years)

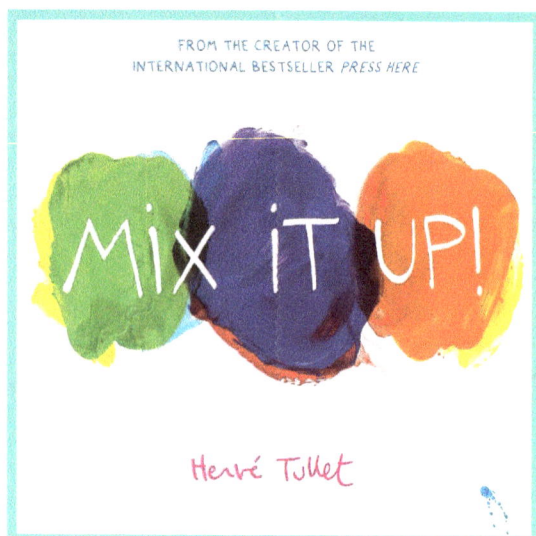

FROM THE CREATOR OF THE
INTERNATIONAL BESTSELLER *PRESS HERE*

MIX iT UP!

Hervé Tullet

An interactive book about colours. Great to lead into an art lesson, particularly when you have access to paint.

- Draw around your hand on white paper then add colour splotches with paint. If you don't have paint, you can still use crayons, textas or pencils to look like the page in the book.

- Make a colour wheel by mixing primary colours to make secondary colours. If you don't have paints, create the colour wheel using coloured pencils or crayons.

- Create folded colour splotches like they do in the book to mix the colours up and see what they change to.

Oi Frog by Kes Gray & Jim Field (All grades)

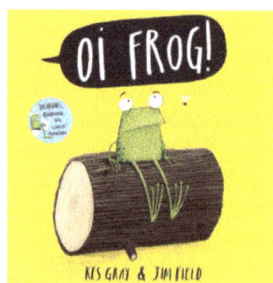

OI FROG!

KES GRAY & JIM FIELD

A hilarious rhyming book with the ridiculous concept that an animal can only sit on something that rhymes with its name!

- Get children to match the animal with the object they could sit on.
- Come up with new animals and objects to match with their name. They could even write and illustrate a new book with their rhyming matches.

- Create your own rhyming poetry with the format of {Animal} [verb] |preposition| (rhyming noun). Eg. Cows sleep on ploughs.
- Practise classification with the animals in the book using habitat, class or food they eat.

This inspirational book covers all the important issues affecting our world and environment.

Themes this book covers that you can discuss and expand on -

- Water
- Sustainability
- Conservation
- Food
- Transport
- Power and its sources
- Housing
- Pollution

- Global warming
- Space
- Hope, awareness and action
- Change and how it affects us

You can find plenty of specific activities in the Teacher's Notes -
http://static.harpercollins.com/harperimages/ommoverride/The_Tomorrow_Book_TN.pdf

The Tomorrow Book by Jackie French (All grades)

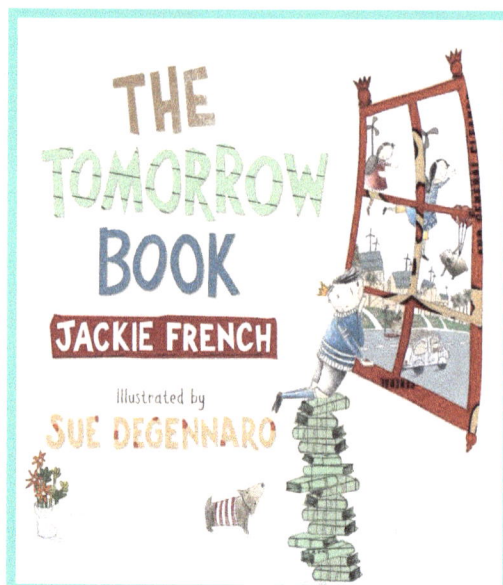

THE TOMORROW BOOK
JACKIE FRENCH
Illustrated by
SUE DEGENNARO

Do Not Open This Book
by Andy Lee (All grades)

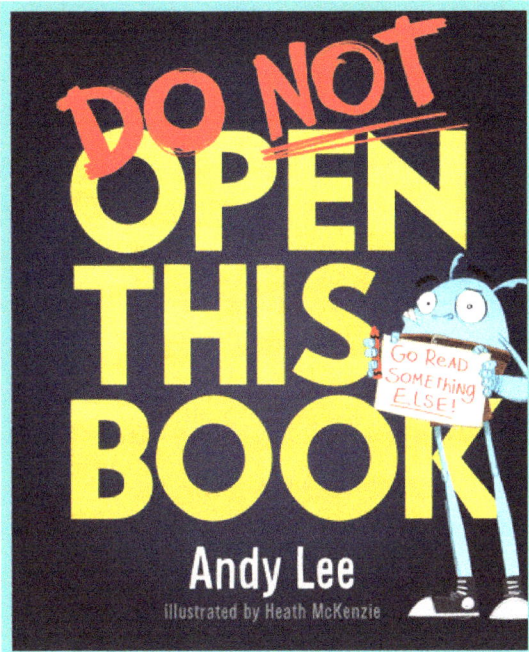

A fun book that has the students calling out in anticipation.

- Get students to come up with a new ending as to what will happen if they get to the last page. Could it be an alien instead of a witch? What else could he turn into?

- Ask students why we kept wanting to turn the page even though we were told not to? Is there any situation they have been in that they have been told not to do something but did it anyway? – Write it down or tell of a situation you were really tempted to do something you were told not to do.

- Discuss what "reverse psychology" is and how it is used in this book. Explain that it is getting somebody to do something you want them to do by suggesting they do the opposite.

Get students to give examples of when it has worked or could work in real life.

Examples
Telling an upset child not to laugh. The child then finds it difficult to keep a straight face.

Telling someone who has given up trying that you knew they couldn't do it. They then try harder to prove that person wrong.

The Day the Crayons Quit
by Drew Daywalt (All grades)

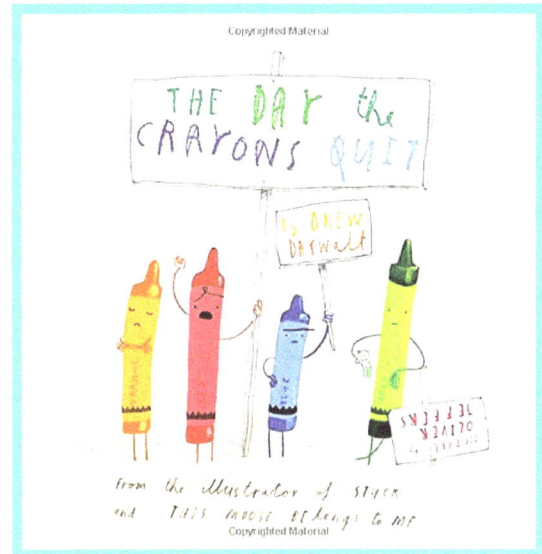

A creative book written from the perspective of a boy's crayons. It is thought provoking, fun and engaging with endless opportunities for activities.

- Get students to write a leader from the perspective of their favourite coloured crayon, to them.

- Draw a picture using unconventional colours to make the crayons happy. Draw a pink sun, purple grass and a blue pig!

- Discuss instances of persuasion throughout the book then get students to write a persuasive text.

Basic outline
- OPINION (I like_____the best.)

- REASON (because_____.)

- EXAMPLE (I can use_____to draw_____.)

- CONCLUSION (_____ is the best crayon in the box.)

A student is tired of their friend never helping out and says "Ok. Don't help. See if I care." The friend decides to help out.

The Gruffalo by Julia Donaldson (All grades)

An engaging rhyming book that sees a mouse outwit its predators with a cunning concept. There are lots of great literacy activities for all ages.

Lower Years
Questions Looking at the cover, where is the story set? What do you think a Gruffalo is? Is it real? What other animals might you find in the woods? Why would the fox/owl/snake want to invite a mouse to tea? Why would the mouse say "No."? Would you like to eat Roasted Fox, Owl Ice cream, Scrambled Snake or Gruffalo Crumble? Why would the Mouse's tummy rumble? Has your tummy rumbled before?
Tricky words Check for understanding of tricky words such as tusks, sped, knobbly knees, turned-out toes, poisonous wart, feast, log-pile house, purple prickles, hid, slid, creature, oh crumbs, astounding, fled.
Draw it Draw or paint a picture of the Gruffalo using the description in the text.
Emotions Discuss the emotions of the characters in the book. How do their expressions change? How are they feeling? Why would they feel like that?
Rhyme Time Get them to predict the rhyming words as you read the text. Get children to come up with different rhyming words.
Punctuate that Observe all the different types of punctuation and explain the use and how it changes our reading voice.
Synonyms "Terrible" has been used lots of times to describe the Gruffalo. Can you think of other synonyms/words to replace "terrible"? Can you find synonyms for any other words in the book?
Write a recipe Write up a recipe for Roasted Fox, Owl ice cream, Scrambled Snake or Gruffalo Crumble. Include Ingredients and Method.
Alliteration Identify the alliteration in the book and get students to come up with more alliteration to suit the story. For example - feisty fox, slippery snake, twisted toes, nasty nose

THE GRUFFALO®

Upper Years
Food Web Put the following animals into a Food Web - mouse, fox, owl, snake, Gruffalo, nuts. Using the concept of the food web, could you think of different characters that could replace the ones in the book?
Dictation Read a sentence or short paragraph aloud and get children to copy it down.
Punctuation Observe the punctuation and font choices and explain why they have been used.
Drama Turn the book into a play. Split into groups of 5, get them to write down their lines as you reread the story and then get them to practice then perform it to the class.
Create your own Gruffalo Create your own Gruffalo and describe and label them using new descriptive words and alliteration.

Suggested websites for interactive resources

If you have access to the Internet use an interactive game or video to help engage the students on the topic they are learning.

All subjects

http://interactivesites.weebly.com
http://splash.abc.net.au/home#!/home
http://www.primaryhomeworkhelp.co.uk
http://www.bbc.co.uk/education
http://getsmarts.weebly.com
http://www.copacabana-ps.com
http://www.crickweb.co.uk
http://pbskids.org
http://www.topmarks.co.uk

Maths

http://au.mathletics.com
Most popular Maths site

http://www.armoredpenguin.com/math/
Maths algorithm generator

http://gregtangmath.com/wordproblems
Maths word problem generator

http://nrich.maths.org
Rich Maths problem

http://www.coolmath-games.com
Fun interactive games

Specialists Lessons

Music
www.musictechteacher.com

PE
www.pecentral.org/websites/kidsites.html
www.physedgames.com
www.pegames.org
www.pecentral.org

LOTE
www.avsystems.com.au/lote-resources
www.education.vic.gov.au/languagesonline

Computer Technology
www.oakdome.com

Favourite Websites

Literacy

http://readingeggs.com.au
Most popular Literacy site

http://resources.woodlands-junior.kent.sch.uk/literacy/
Interactive games

www.roythezebra.com/
Guided Reading games for Lower Primary

www.pobble365.com
Writing stimulus ideas

www.abc.net.au/btn
Behind the News- news stories for students

Helpful Resources

http://www.storylineonline.net
Stories read by celebrities

http://www.literacyshed.com
Themed filmclips and lessons

https://storyboxlibrary.com.au
($29.95 annual membership)

www.wingclips.com
Inspiring movie clips

www.kidsloveshortfilms.com
Movies for wet lunches

http://gonoodle.com
Great for brain breaks

Supply Resources

http://www.teacherneedhelp.com/
students/subtch.htm

http://reliefteachingideas.com
Facebook community

http://www.reliefteaching.com

http://www.supplybag.co.uk

TIPS

THINGS TO HAVE IN YOUR SUPPLY BAG

Teacher for a Day
How to Get Started, Engage Students and Succeed as a Supply, Relief or Substitute Teacher

Hat
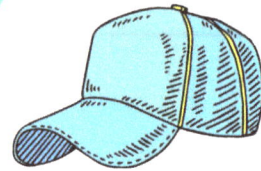

Water Bottle

Whistle

Pens

Watch

USB
for saved resources, music and movies.

Lead Pencils and Erasers for Students

Stickers and/or a Stamp

2 Dice

Blank A4 paper

in case the classroom doesn't have any. Cut in half and use both sides for activities if possible to make it last longer.

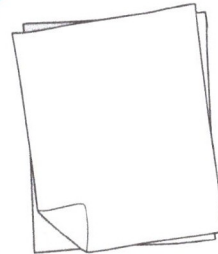

Grid paper/book

useful for word search activities, and other suggested maths activities in this book.

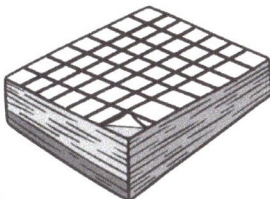

Hacky sack/Foam Ball

for silent ball or to get students to answer questions.

Education is the most powerful weapon you can use to change the world.

-Nelson Mandela

Organiser

SCHOOL CONTACT DETAILS

School _____

Address _____

_____

Phone _____

Email _____

Principal _____

Deputy Principal _____

HR Staff _____

School _____

Address _____

_____

Phone _____

Email _____

Principal _____

Deputy Principal _____

HR Staff _____

School _____

Address _____

_____

Phone _____

Email _____

Principal _____

Deputy Principal _____

HR Staff _____

School _____

Address _____

_____

Phone _____

Email _____

Principal _____

Deputy Principal _____

HR Staff _____

School _____

Address _____

_____

Phone _____

Email _____

Principal _____

Deputy Principal _____

HR Staff _____

School _____

Address _____

_____

Phone _____

Email _____

Principal _____

Deputy Principal _____

HR Staff _____

SCHOOL YEAR CALENDAR

Term 1	Monday	Tuesday	Wednesday	Thursday	Friday
1					
2					
3					
4					
5					
6					
7					
8					
9					
10					
11					

Term 2	Monday	Tuesday	Wednesday	Thursday	Friday
1					
2					
3					
4					
5					
6					
7					
8					
9					
10					
11					

Record your school bookings over the year.

Term 3	Monday	Tuesday	Wednesday	Thursday	Friday
1					
2					
3					
4					
5					
6					
7					
8					
9					
10					
11					

Term 4	Monday	Tuesday	Wednesday	Thursday	Friday
1					
2					
3					
4					
5					
6					
7					
8					
9					
10					
11					

IMPORTANT DATES

New Years Day
January 1

Australia Day
January 26

Chinese New Year
January 28

Waitangi Day
February 6

Valentines Day
February 14

Clean Up Australia Day
March 5

St. Patrick's Day
March 17

Harmony Day
March 21

April Fool's Day
April 1

Good Friday
April 14

Easter Sunday
April 16

Anzac Day
April 25

Mother's Day
May 14

Red Nose Day
June 30

NAIDOC Week
July 2

USA's Independence Day
July 4

Jeans for Genes Day
August 4

Father's Day
September 3

R U OK Day
September 14

World Mental Health Day
October 10

Halloween
October 31

Remembrance Day
November 11

Hanukkah
December 13

Christmas Day
December 25

New Year's Eve
December 31

SCHOOL TERMS AND HOLIDAY DATES

1st Term	
Term 1	Public or other holidays
School Holidays	

2nd Term	
Term 2	Public or other holidays
School Holidays	

3rd Term	
Term 3	Public or other holidays
School Holidays	

4th Term	
Term 4	Public or other holidays
School Holidays	

TEACHING EXPENSES FOR 20_

Keep all receipts and this Log Book for Tax Time

Tip: Take a photo of receipts and upload to a Tax Receipts App

Date	Resources Equipment, Computer and Phones, Materials and Supplies, Stationery, Prizes, Workbag	Shop Officeworks, Kmart etc.	Cost

Date	Clothing Logo only, Protective wear, Sun Protection, Dry Cleaning	Cost

Date	Professional Development Courses, Costs for Excursions or Camps	Cost

Date	Professional Fees Unions, Registrations, Memberships, Subscriptions	Cost

Date	Travel Travel Expenses, Car Usage, Excursion or Camp Expenses	Kms or Cost

Date	Home Office Phone, Internet and Electricity Usage	Cost

PROFESSIONAL DEVELOPMENT RECORDS

Date	Course	Company

Remember to keep certificates, notes and proof of your courses.

Hours	Standards	Notes

Some places to find Professional Development courses as a Supply Teacher.

• Your state's Teacher Governing Body will have many free online courses including Student Protection, Code of Conduct, Behaviour Management. etc.

• Supply Teacher Association gives you access to up to 30 hours of accredited PD and other support for $99/year. This is a lot cheaper than paying to go to courses.

• Ask schools you regularly attend if you can attend some of their PD courses.

Education's purpose is to replace an empty
mind with an open one.

-Malcolm Forbes

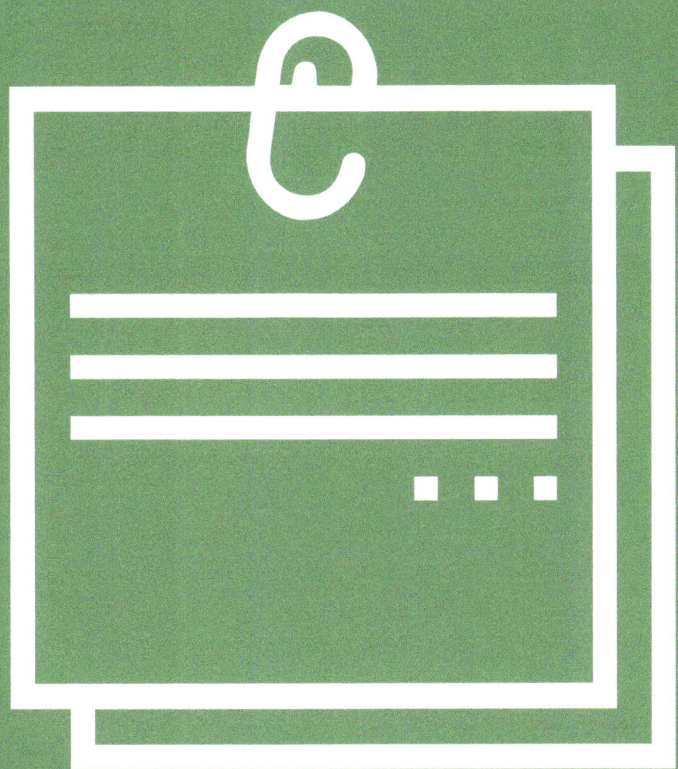

Daily Plan and Notes

A suggested daily plan if no plan is left.

Please refer to activities listed throughout this book for an elaboration on those suggested in the below plans.

PREP/KINDERGARTEN

DAILY PLAN AND NOTES

Morning Session	
Before Class	Put out puzzles, drawing, blocks etc. for when students first come in for the day.
Introduction	Mark roll, tuckshop, homework, revise class rules/rewards/behaviour management systems
Literacy Rotations 10-15 minute rotations	1. Sight words- write sentences 2. Handwriting 3. Reading- read a book then write 5+ words and draw a picture for the word OR write down all the words that start with… S. 4. Missing Sounds *Use Interactive White Board as a rotation if possible
Spelling	Pizza in your face game using sight words
Break	Brain Food/Game
Read a story	As a class read a story
Reading activity	Choose 5 words to write and illustrate. Teacher writes on the board for students to copy.
Pack up	Pack up early to go out for Lunch
First Break	
Counting	Count as a class in 1's, 2's, 5's, 10's forwards and backwards to 100.
Maths Rotations	1. Sums on the board. Copy, use pop sticks etc then draw objects to show working. 2. Make patterns with unifix then draw. 3. Puzzles/Maths board games in the room. 4. Playdough make shapes or numbers. *Use Interactive White Board as a rotation if possible
Maths activity	Guess a number
Pack up	Pack up early to go out for Lunch
Second break	
	Mark roll Read a book to the class
Art activity	Draw a Clown and Monster
Game	Minute Mime
Pack up	Stack chairs, close windows, tidy floor, wipe board

Activity table rotations are common in Prep classes. Get the teacher aide's advice on what works best with the class. Use lots of explicit direction and modelling for everything. Keep them moving, between floor work and their desks. Activities should go for 15-30 minutes. Use lots of positive praise to reinforce good behaviour. Acknowledge those doing the right thing and watch the other children quickly do the same.

Morning Session	
Before Class	Set up chairs and pencils etc. for the day.
Introduction	Mark roll, tuckshop, homework, revise class rules/rewards/behaviour management systems.
Writing	Write a list- 10 favourite things
Spelling	Missing Sounds
Break	Stretching
Read a story	As a class read a story
Reading Comprehension	Draw and write what happens in the beginning, middle and ending of the story.
First Break	
Counting	Hundreds Board- Even and Odd
Number	Adding Dice
Maths	Grid Coordinates
Game	Corners
Second break	
	Mark roll Read a book to the class
Art	Directional Drawing- Lion
Speaking	Show and Tell
Pack up	Stack chairs, close windows, tidy floor, wipe board

YEAR 1/2

DAILY PLAN AND NOTES

Morning Session	
Introduction	Mark roll, tuckshop, homework, revise class rules/rewards/behaviour management systems
Spelling	Back to Front Spelling
Spelling Activity	Write sentences using spelling words
Writing	Write instructions on how to make a pizza
Break	Brain Food/Game
Read a story	As a class read a story- omit the ending
Reading activity	Predict the ending of the story. Write and draw your prediction.
Game	Stop! Go!
Handwriting	Next page of Handwriting book
First Break	
Maths intro	More and Less
Algorithms	Word problems
Game	Guess the Number
Maths activity	Follow directions
Second break	
	Mark roll Read a book to the class
Art activity	Crumpled Paper Art
Game	Pizza Massage
Pack up	Stack chairs, close windows, tidy floor, wipe board

This age group will need lots of modelling for each activity. Give lots of explicit direction and examples. Activities should only last around 30 minutes. Do whole class explanations on the carpet then back to desks for their activity. Be sure to use lots of positive praise for Behaviour Management. Most children are still keen to please at this age.

Morning Session	
Introduction	Mark roll, tuckshop, homework, revise class rules/rewards/behaviour management systems
Writing	Persuasive Text
Spelling	Dice Spelling
Break	Yoga
Read a story	Students read a book (or teacher can)
Reading	Book Review
Speaking	I went to the shop
First Break	
Maths intro	Hundred's Chart- Missing Number
Maths	Graphing
Number	Dice Activities- Roll a Monster
Game	Around the World
Second break	
	Mark roll Read a book to the class
Art	Draw a Poem
Game	Heads Down, Thumbs Up
Pack up	Stack chairs, close windows, tidy floor, wipe board

YEAR 3/4

Morning Session	
Introduction	Mark roll, tuckshop, homework, revise class rules/rewards/behaviour management systems
Spelling	Write out spelling words
Spelling Activity	Write sentences using spelling words Alphabetical order (Fast Finishers)
Writing	Write a recipe for your dream dessert
Break	Brain Food/Game
Read a story	Read a story to the class
Reading activity	Design a new cover for the book
Grammar	Super Sentences
Game	Heads down, thumbs up
First Break	
Maths intro	Mad Minute
Algorithms	Sums on the board or word problems
Game	Around the World
Maths activity	Robot Maths
Second break	
	Mark roll Silent Reading
Art activity	Textured Landscape
Speaking & Listening	Nursery Rhyme Mix-up
Pack up	Stack chairs, close windows, tidy floor, wipe board

This age group can work more independently and activities should go from 30-45 minutes. Students become more aware of their peers and can become more defiant, especially if a task is too challenging. Make sure your activities are achievable for the majority and be there to assist those that are struggling. Use a game or activity they like to keep them motivated and on task.

Morning Session	
Introduction	Mark roll, tuckshop, homework, revise class rules/rewards/behaviour management systems
Writing	Persuasive Text
Spelling	Find a Word
Break	Mirror, Mirror
Read a story	Read a story to the class
Reading activity	Write a new ending
Game	The Never-Ending Sentence
First Break	
Maths intro	Maths Bingo
Number	Roll and Round it
Maths	Follow Directions
Game	Dollar Dice
Second break	
	Mark roll Read a book to the class
Art	Magazine Tearing
Game	Dots and Boxes
Pack up	Stack chairs, close windows, tidy floor, wipe board

YEAR 5/6

Morning Session	
Introduction	Mark roll, tuckshop, homework, revise class rules/rewards/behaviour management systems
Spelling	Alphabetical Order
Spelling Activity	Spelling Money activity
Writing	Write a letter to someone you miss
Break	Brain Food/Game
Read a story	Students read individually
Reading activity	Book review Copy 10 words from the book and write them in alphabetical order. (Fast Finishers)
Word work	Word in a word
Game	The Never Ending Sentence
First Break	
Algorithms	Sums on the board or word problems
Time	Daily Schedule
Maths Activity	Follow Directions
Game	Greedy Pig
Second break	
	Mark roll Silent Reading
Art	Zentangle Hands
Speaking	Topic talk
Pack up	Stack chairs, close windows, tidy floor, wipe board

This age group can work independently and lessons can be sustained for 40-60 minutes. Be mindful of peer approval and give more subtle praise to avoid 'embarrassment.' Make sure you are firm but fair and follow through with consequences. Bribe them with a game or activity they like to keep them on task.

Morning Session	
Introduction	Mark roll, tuckshop, homework, revise class rules/rewards/behaviour management systems
Literacy	Creative Product Launch
Break	Mindful Meditation
Writing	Super Stories
Spelling	Edit a Sentence
Game	Scattegories
First Break	
Maths intro	Rounding
Maths	Dice Activity - Fraction Order
Maths	Calculator Words
Game	Game of Greed
Second break	
	Mark roll Silent Reading
Art	Line and Colour
Game	Grandma's Undies
Pack up	Stack chairs, close windows, tidy floor, wipe board

DAILY PLAN

Morning Session	
Introduction	Mark roll, tuckshop, homework, revise class rules/rewards/behaviour management systems
Break	Brain Food/Game
First Break	
Second break	
	Mark roll Reading to the class or silently
Pack up	Stack chairs, close windows, tidy floor, wipe board

DATE: _____

SUPPLY TEACHER:

_____

_____

CONTACT:

_____

WHILE YOU WERE OUT

OVERALL CLASS BEHAVIOUR

☆☆☆☆☆

SUPERSTAR STUDENTS

STUDENTS NEEDING REMINDERS

NOTES

DAILY PLAN AND NOTES

NOTES

NOTES

Tell me and I'll forget; show me and I may remember; involve me and I'll understand.

-Chinese proverb

Literacy

LOWER PRIMARY

📖 READING

Using a suitable book students can-

• Predict the ending and write or draw it.

• Draw and write what happens at the beginning, middle and ending of the story.

• Write a list of 10 things in the book, and then draw them or describe what they are e.g. a house is a building in which you live.

• Choose 5 words to write and illustrate.

• Character Analysis- What does the character look like, act like and do in the story? Break the page up into quarters and have them fill in- Appearance, Personality, Actions and Picture.

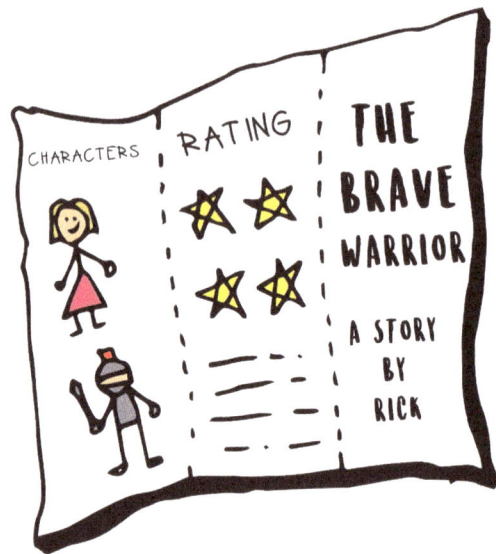

Book Review

Fold a blank A4 piece of paper in thirds. On one side students write Beginning, Middle, Ending. They will draw a picture and write about each. On the back they have the cover page, book name and picture, characters and setting and then the rating (5 stars). Once folded it looks like a brochure.

✏️ WRITING

Writing prompts

Recount
- On the weekend I did (or didn't do)...
- My favourite holiday ever...
- For my last birthday...

Procedure
Write instructions on -
- How to make a sundae.
- How to make a Monster Milkshake.
- How to wash your hair.
- How to build a sandcastle.
- How to make a magic potion.

Persuasive
Remember to encourage persuasive and emotive language.
- Imagine you found a hippo in your backyard. Should you keep it or give it to the zoo? Why?
- What is the best superpower to have? Why?
- If you could go anywhere in the world, where you would go? Why?
- Families are important because...

Letter
- Write a letter to your teacher or a loved one.
- Write a letter to a stranger telling them about yourself.
- Write a letter to the principal with suggestions you think would improve the school.

List
Write a list of -
- Food you would like on your shopping list to eat at home.
- What your 10 favourite things are (Eg. Food, sport, hobbies, toys, places, activities etc.).
- What you would like for your next birthday.
- People in your family.

Narrative
- Pobble 365 (www.pobble365.com) or picture writing stimulus on page 117 or 118
- One day a spaceship landed in my backyard and ...
- Write a story about something strange found inside a cupboard. It could be another world or room, a lost treasure, a time machine, a person or animal.

Description
Using adjectives, their senses and detailed language, describe -
- The school playground at lunchtime.
- Your first day of school.
- A day at the beach.
- The first time you went to a sweets store.

63

LITERACY

Roll a Story

Roll the dice to determine the story features, then write a narrative based around them.

	Roll 1 **Character**	Roll 2 **Setting**	Roll 3 **Problem**
●	A courageous woman	on a farm	found an unlucky charm
●●	A grumpy old man	at a themepark	lost something important
●●	A kind-hearted boy	in an aeroplane	was sent back in time
●● ●●	An energetic girl	at the beach	was caught in a trap
●●● ●●	An evil doctor	in an old cottage	was in a terrible accident
●●● ●●●	A dangerous animal	in the forest	got stuck in a dreadful storm

Poetry

Alliteration, Acrostic or Shape Poem on unit/holiday/names or any themes.

Alliteration

Andy Ant ate all the apples.

Dean dropped a dirty dog.

Mighty Mark makes milkshakes.

Acrostic

Dude
Awesome
Nice
Intelligent
Energetic
Lovely

Shape

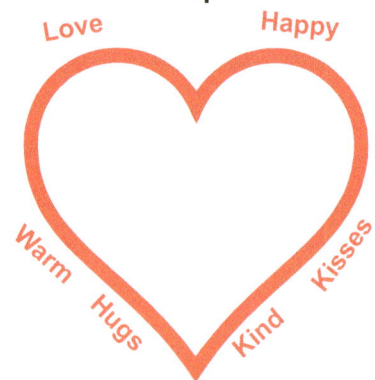

Love   Happy

Warm   Hugs   Kind   Kisses

Handwriting

If students don't have a handwriting workbook, do something similar to the handwriting they have done previously in their books.

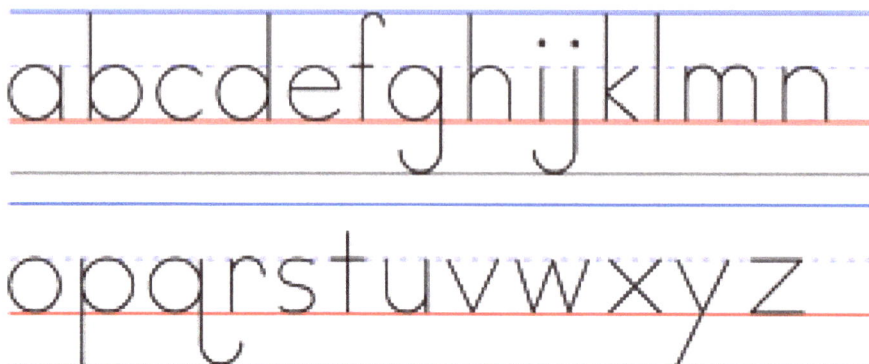

abcdefghijklmn

opqrstuvwxyz

A✓ SPELLING

Using students spelling words/sight words/ themed words

Sentences
Students write sentences using their spelling words.

Draw a Picture
Draw a picture to accompany each spelling word.

Back to Front
Students write words forwards and then backwards.

Dictation
Teacher reads sentences using spelling words and students copy them down.

Cloze Activity

Write sentences on the board and omit a spelling word in each. On the other side of the board, list the missing words and outline the shape of the letter or write the number of letters spaces for Prep/ Year 1 students. Students then have to copy the sentences and fill in the missing words.

Eg. The _ _ _ loved playing with his dog.
Blue _ _ my favourite colour.
I go shopping _ _ _ _ my Mum.
I have a red _ _ _.

with   hat   boy   is

Dice Spelling

Each dice number has a different instruction for their spelling words.

⚀ **Rainbow colours**
⚁ **SILLy writing**
⚂ **Blue vowels**
⚃ **Red consonants**
⚄ **ALL CAPITAL letters**
⚅ **AB colour pattern**

Pizza in your face

Going around in a circle students spell a given word, one letter per student. If the student says the wrong letter they sit down. At the end of the word the teacher in the middle says "Pizza.. in.. your.. face" pointing to a child per word. The child that lands on "face" has to sit down and the remaining students go on to spell the next word until one child is remaining.

PIZZA
FACE!
YOUR
IN

65

LITERACY

ABC GRAMMAR

Edit a sentence

Write sentences with spelling, punctuation and grammatical errors for students to rewrite correctly.

are yoo redy four bed.
(5 mistakes)

Are you ready for bed?

on sonday we went two the beech
(6 mistakes)

On Sunday we went to the beach.

mi best frend is ben
(5 mistakes)

My best friend is Ben.

bof our birfdays is in june
(6 mistakes)

Both our birthdays are in June.

when is ti hom tim.
(5 mistakes)

When is it home time ?

i luv eatn froot
(5 mistakes)

I love eating fruit.

Super Sentences

Build on a sentence by- adding an ending, adding a beginning, adding an adjective, adverb, alliteration, simile etc.

Examples:

The dog ate the bone.

The **lonely** dog ate the bone.

The **playful** puppy ate the **meaty** bone.

Sentence Suggestions

The house was on fire.

The girl rode her bike.

A car crashed into a tree.

A lion walked.

The lady screamed.

The man jumped.

WORD WORK

Missing Sounds

Choose a focus sound to work on. Students fill in the missing letter to complete the word then draw a picture of the word.

Eg. Focus sound a-   h_t   f_n   c_p

Blends and Word Families

Focus on a blend or word family and students create words and draw pictures for each.

🟧 **Blends**   🟥 **Word Families**

bl	br	ch	ck	cl	cr	dr	fl	fr	gh
gl	gr	ng	ph	pl	pr	qu	sc	sh	sk
sl	sm	sn	sp	st	sw	th	tr	tw	wh
wr	ack	ain	ake	ale	all	ame	an	ank	ap
ash	at	ate	aw	ay	eat	ell	en	est	et
ice	ick	ide	ight	ill	in	ine	ing	ink	ip
it	ock	oke	op	ore	ot	uck	ug	ump	unk

Letter find

Students write out the alphabet then identify the letter with the teacher's clues.

Examples:

Letter that comes before…

Write the next 2 letters after…

Write the previous 2 letters before…

Circle the letter between…

Underline the 3rd letter.

Cross out the 15th letter.

Change a letter

Write a 3- or 4-letter word on the board then students come up and change one letter to create a new word. You could give them restrictions to focus on certain sounds e.g., only change the first letter- _at…hat, cat, or keep the vowel sound e.g., mop, top, tot, cot, cop, etc.

🗣 SPEAKING AND LISTENING

Show and Tell

Students stand in front of the class and either show the class something or tell them about something.

I went to the shop

Students sit in a circle and name things that they bought at the shop. Each student has to recall what the previous students have said. E.g., 'I went to the shop and I bought…. an apple.' Next 'I went to the shop and I bought…an apple and a cake.'

Draw a Poem

Students follow the poem's instructions to draw each character.

Draw a Robot

When drawing a robot it is said
Always start with
a square shaped head.

From his face he needs to see
So draw two eyes
that stare squarely.

He needs a mouth to talk to you
A rectangle will do,
colour it too.

You will want to give orders
so he needs to hear
On each side of his head,
draw him a robot ear.

We need an antenna
on top of his head
Draw a wire with a ball
so information will imbed.

Underneath you can draw
his torso - strong
Sketch an oblong body
and you can't go wrong.

Then he needs some arms
so draw them, long
Now he can help grab
and pull things along.

Don't forget to add his hands,
to help him grab at things
Sketch him two robotic pincers
and see what objects he now
brings.

For him to move around,
he needs something
steady down below
So, draw some legs
or wheels for feet
Slow or fast,
now he can go, go, go!

Check out your cool, new robot
I must say he's looking pretty neat
Now you can colour him in
to make him look finished
and complete.

Draw an Elephant

When drawing an elephant it is said
Always start with a big, round head.

On each side she needs to hear
So draw a humongous, elephant ear.

This special thing makes her stand out
Draw a long trunk from where water can spout.

To make sure she can see where she goes
Draw two little eyes above her nose.

Draw a big circle, extra round.
She's the heaviest animal on top of the ground.

Underneath her body do you know what goes?
Four stumpy legs with three big toes.

Behind her bottom she needs a swishy tail
So other elephants can hold on in a trail.

You've drawn your elephant from head to feet
Now colour her in, nice and neat.

We can't forget what everyone knows
Is he must have a red, round nose

His mouth is as wide as
the River Nile
So draw for him a
humungous smile.

Draw his body,
his arms and hands
Add orange gloves that look so grand

He needs some legs to help him stroll
Make them long and skinny like a pole

Draw him an outfit that looks mighty fine
He loves a onesie with a colourful design

For his feet, here's some clues
He needs some big, goofy clown shoes

On his shirt he wears a trick flower
If you get too close it will give you a
shower

I hope you listened to every rule
And now your clown is looking cool.

Draw a Clown

When drawing a clown it is said
You must begin with his
big round head

He wants attention
so people will stare
So give him colourful, curly hair

He wants to hear people
laugh and cheer
So on each side of his head
give him an ear.

To make sure he can see what to do
Draw for him bright eyes, coloured
blue

Draw a Monster

When you draw a monster, it is said
You must begin with a funny-shaped head.

He'll be able to see in the night skies
If we draw him three googly eyes

Our monster will have a big, ugly nose
With green boogers coming out like a hose

He needs a mouth so he can eat
All the children's smelly feet

Now up the top and underneath
This monster needs lots of sharp teeth

Just below we need to check
That we don't forget to draw his neck

Our monster is big and his belly is too
So let's draw his large body blue

To make him look a little scary
He needs some arms that are hairy

Some legs are needed to make him move
Choose how many to make him groove.

To help him walk down the street
He will need some big, stinky feet

Now it's time to make your monster unique
Add something scary that will make
everyone shriek!

LITERACY

FAST FINISHERS

Read a book
Silently read a book.

Life or Death
Write down 5 things you could not live without. Write 5 things you could live without.

Grocery List
Write down your ideal grocery list with anything you would like on it.

Dear Friend
Write a letter or make a card for a friend or relative.

UPPER PRIMARY

📖 READING

Using a suitable book students can -
- Write a new ending.

- Copy 10 words from the book then put them in alphabetical order.

- Find 10 challenging words and write down the dictionary meaning.

- Find 10 words and write the antonym and synonym for each.

- Design a new cover.

- Rewrite the story from the perspective of a different character.

- Write a letter to the author.

- Change the gender of the characters and show how the story would be different. Discuss gender differences as a class.

Book Review

Fold a blank A4 piece of paper into thirds. On one side students write Beginning, Middle, Ending. They will draw a picture and write about each. On the back they have the cover page, book name and picture, characters and setting and then the rating (5 stars). Once folded it looks like a brochure. Refer to page 62 for the layout.

Character Analysis

What does the character look like, act like and do in the story? Break the page up into quarters and have them fill in Appearance, Personality, Actions and Picture (to draw). Students can also give evidence from the book for each.

Appearance	Personality
Actions	Picture

✏️ WRITING

Writing prompts

Narrative

- Pobble 365 (www.pobble365.com) or picture writing stimulus on page 117 or 118
- Write a story about children who live in a strange world where there is no technology, no T.V., no iPads, no computers, no phones. What will they do?
- Tell a story about a day in which everything goes wrong.
- Imagine you woke up one morning and you had switched bodies with someone or something (eg. an animal). What would you do? Write a story about your day.

Recount

- My most memorable holiday ever…
- The best birthday ever…
- The best day in my life was…

Procedure

Write instructions on-

- How to make your dream dessert.
- How to care for a pet.
- How to get to your house from school.
- How to make an edible treat for a bad guy.
- How to play a game (like silent ball, heads down thumbs up).

Persuasive Writing

Introductions
I think...
For this reason...
I feel that...
I am sure that...

Endings
For these reasons...
As you can see...
In other words...
On the whole...

Making Your Point
Firstly, secondly, thirdly...
Because...
Furthermore...
In addition...

Other Words
reasons
arguments
for
against
unfair
pros
cons

Details
For example...
In fact...
For instance...
As evidence...

Persuasive

- Should we reduce our time at school each week? Why or why not?
- Write a review on your favourite movie or book.
- Create an advertisement for a new drink or food brand.
- Write a letter convincing your principal of changes you think are needed around the school.
- Can screen time influence your behaviour? How? Should parents restrict screen time?
- Should children have to do chores around the house or school? Why or why not?
- If I ever have children I will never…

Letter

Write a letter to -

- Someone you miss.
- Your hero.
- Your best friend.
- Your teacher about ways he/she could improve your days at school.
- A journal entry as yourself or as a fictional character you create.

List

Write a list of -

- 10 things you are grateful for that cost less than $5.
- A shopping list with all the food you like.
- The advantages and disadvantages of having grass in your house instead of carpet or tiles.
- The pros and cons of being a girl/boy.

Description

Use adjectives, their senses and detailed language to describe -

- Features of a particular animal.
- The room you are in.
- Your life as a dog.
- A day at a theme park.
- Where you live (city/town) as if it were a person - *Eg. The Gold Coast is like a crazy party animal. He loves to play and beach all day then party all night.*

Information Report

Research a topic and set out a report with an Introduction, Paragraphs and Subheadings and Images. Some topic ideas could be -

- What is/was life like for...a gladiator, a refugee, an explorer, a prisoner at Alcatraz etc.
- How does _____ work? A telephone, a GPS, a computer, electricity etc.
- What is being done to protect...endangered wildlife, the environment, minorities and people at risk, refugees?
- How and why were cats and dogs domesticated?
- Write an autobiography of your life so far.

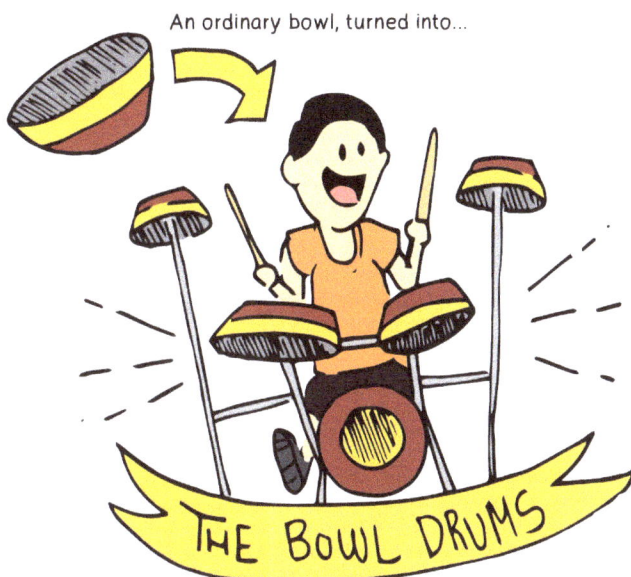

Creative Product Launch

Get students to create a new use for an everyday item. They then need to write about its new use and draw it in action. Then they can design a print advertisement/poster and come up with other ways they are going to launch their product.

An example is-

- Breakfast bowl being used as a musical instrument or a cockroach catcher etc.

Some everyday item suggestions- pencil, milk bottle, hat, fork, shoe, book etc.

75

LITERACY

Newspaper Scavenger Hunt

Use a copy of a newspaper and see how many of the following you can find.

1. The price of the newspaper
2. The World News page number
3. Number of pages
4. The date the newspaper was published/printed
5. Minimum and maximum temperatures in your capital city
6. Lead headline
7. Lead story
8. A caption
9. A political cartoon
10. An ad with a slogan
11. A synonym for happy
12. An interesting verb from a headline
13. Five adjectives in one story
14. A noun in a headline that is not a person or a place
15. An item for sale under $5
16. A new car for sale under $20,000
17. A picture of someone who is happy
18. A number greater than 200
19. A form of transport
20. The first letter of your name
21. A question mark (?)
22. A cartoon character
23. The page of the editorial
24. Something that uses electricity
25. Pictures of 2 different sports
26. Something to eat
27. Newspaper index
28. A word that describes Queensland
29. A house for rent under $500/week
30. A new word to add to your vocabulary
31. A news story about a crisis
32. A human interest news story
33. A display ad that contains an opinion
34. Page number of the first full page display ad
35. An item for sale that is seasonal
36. An ad designed for young people
37. The cost of 1kg of meat
38. The latest result for a current sporting event
39. A classified ad selling a dog
40. A person to whom you would write a letter

Story Starters

• I couldn't believe my ears when they called to tell me the news.

• There was a time that I was extremely happy.

• I was about to start my first day of high school and I was far from excited.

• The scent of home-baked biscuits wafted through the room and it immediately reminded me of home.

• John couldn't think of anything other than his little sister, who had been missing for 22 hours now.

• Onlookers' faces dropped as they witnessed a plane falling out of the sky and exploding in a blaze of fire.

• Peta knew this audition was her last chance to get her big break.

Sizzling starts

• Frantically I/he/she/we…

• Really? What a disaster…

• I stared in amazement…

• I couldn't believe my ears…

Handwriting

If students don't have a handwriting workbook, do something similar to the handwriting they have done previously.

Super Stories

Using a piece of paper, students write a story introduction then fold it over and switch with someone. Repeat this by next writing a complication, resolution and conclusion. At the end, open up piece of paper and read the story outline.

Poetry

Alliteration, Acrostic or Shape Poem on unit/holiday/names or any themes.

Acrostic

S ports
C lasstime
H olidays
O rder tuckshop
O val
L earning

Poetry Slam

Watch videos and get students to write a rap or slam about something they are passionate about.

Shape

Green leaves growing

Trees swaying in the wind

Yellow leaves falling

Alliteration

A slippery snake slithered into the snow.

Makenna may munch on mandarins on Monday.

A ginormous gorilla named Gordon gracefully grazed on grapes.

On Saturday, a sweet, sassy salesperson called Sophia showed me to the stylish suits.

A✓ SPELLING

Using students' spelling words/sight words/themed words

• **Sentences** • **Dictionary Meanings** • **Alphabetical order**

DUCK - BLACK - JACK
SHACK - CLOCK - WHACK

Dictation

Teacher reads sentences using spelling words and students write them down.

Find a word

Use grid paper to create a find a word using your spelling words. Swap with a partner and find their words.

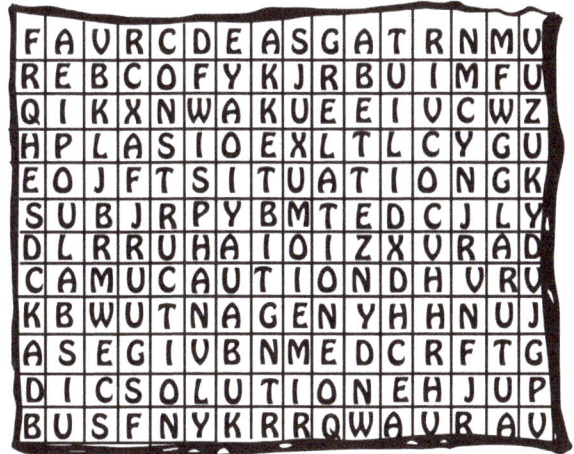

F	A	V	R	C	D	E	A	S	G	A	T	R	N	M	V
R	E	B	C	O	F	Y	K	J	R	B	U	I	M	F	U
Q	I	K	X	N	W	A	K	U	E	E	I	V	C	W	Z
H	P	L	A	S	I	O	E	X	L	T	L	C	Y	G	U
E	O	J	F	T	S	I	T	U	A	T	I	O	N	G	K
S	U	B	J	R	P	Y	B	M	T	E	D	C	J	L	Y
D	L	R	R	U	H	A	I	O	I	Z	X	V	R	A	D
C	A	M	U	C	A	U	T	I	O	N	D	H	V	R	U
K	B	W	U	T	N	A	G	E	N	Y	H	H	N	U	J
A	S	E	G	I	V	B	N	M	E	D	C	R	F	T	G
D	I	C	S	O	L	U	T	I	O	N	E	H	J	U	P
B	U	S	F	N	Y	K	R	R	Q	W	A	V	R	A	V

Spelling Money

If each letter is worth an amount A=$1 B=$2 C=$3…Z=$26 how much would each of your spelling words be worth? Students can then do it for their name, find a word that is worth $100 etc.

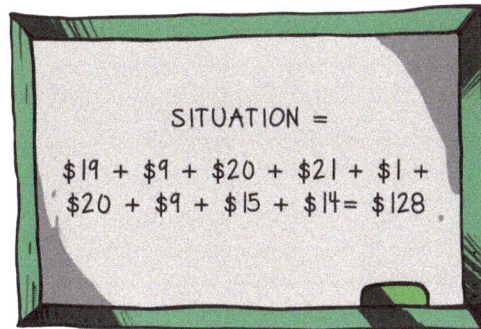

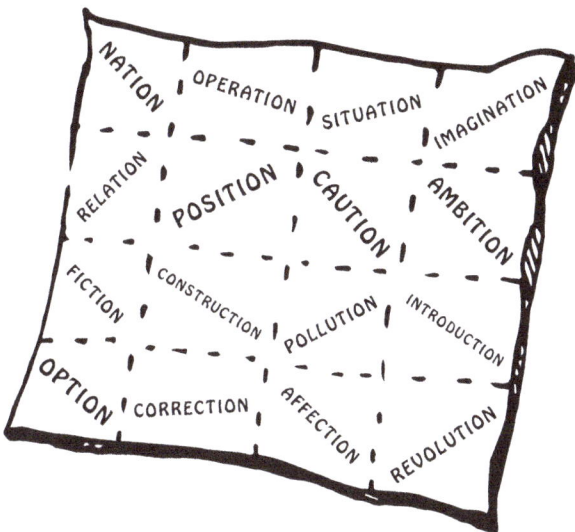

SITUATION =

$19 + $9 + $20 + $21 + $1 + $20 + $9 + $15 + $14 = $128

NATION OPERATION SITUATION IMAGINATION
RELATION POSITION CAUTION AMBITION
FICTION CONSTRUCTION POLLUTION INTRODUCTION
OPTION CORRECTION AFFECTION REVOLUTION

Spelling Bingo

Students fold a piece of paper to create 16 sections, and put their spelling words into squares randomly. Teacher calls out words and students mark them off. The first student to stand up and call out their spelling words correctly, wins.

79

LITERACY

ABC GRAMMAR

Edit a sentence

Write sentences on the board with spelling, punctuation and grammatical errors for students to rewrite correctly. (#) is the number of mistakes in each line.

1. joanna forgot her book last wensday four her report (5)

Joanna forgot her book last Wednesday for her report.

2. I wood much rathur have my freind over then go too church (6)

I would much rather have my friend over than go to church.

3. michael jaxson is probabley the most famouse performer of the centuary (7)

Michael Jackson is probably the most famous performer off the century.

4. my mom kath luvs goin two tennis every weekend with her frend leone. (7)

My mum Kath loves going to tennis every weekend with her friend Leone.

5. lisa cryed I think my knew jackit has been stoled (8)

Lisa cried, "I think my new jacket has been stolen ! "

6. sarah asked does anywon no how much the tickits cost (8)

Sarah asked, " Does anyone know how much the tickets cost? "

7. who meny studants will bee coming two the disco inquired rebecca (10)

" How many students will be coming to the disco? " inquired Rebecca.

8. have you herd off the to bodys of water called the mississippi river and the nile (10)

Have you heard of the two bodies of water called the Mississippi River and The Nile?

9. i no most of the countrees and capittals of the werld ansered the inteligent forth grader (12)

" I know most of the countries and capitals of the world. " answered the intelligent fourth grader.

10. why dont you call youre frend said mum becose we had a teribble fite i replyed. (18)

"Why don't you call your friend?" said Mum. "Because we had a terrible fight, " I replied.

Super Sentences

Build on a sentence by- adding an ending, adding a beginning, adding an adjective, adverb, alliteration, simile etc. to create a complex sentence.

Examples:

The dog ate the bone.

All through the night the dog **chewed on** the bone.

The dog **quietly gnawed on** the bone **while we all ate our dinner.**

Sentence Suggestions

The house was on fire.   A lion walked.

The girl rode her bike.   The lady screamed.

A car crashed into a tree. The man jumped.

SPEAKING AND LISTENING

Topic Recall

Choose a topic eg. boy's/girl's/people's names, healthy food, animals, fruit, vehicles, celebrities, songs, etc. Going around the class/circle students say one answer then repeat the people before them. Eg. boys names- Adam… Adam, Daniel… Adam, Daniel, Evan etc. You could also do it in alphabetical order.

The Never-ending Sentence

Students say one word at a time and continue a sentence using connectives (and, like, but, then, next, finally, later, before, so, since, because, however, finally, therefore, yet, furthermore, accordingly, consequently, similarly etc.). Brainstorm and write up connectives on the board to help.

Topic Talk

Students talk on a given or chosen topic for 1 minute trying not to say "um". Keep tally of how many "ums" are said and the winner is the student with the least "ums".

Friends

Recycling

Should we have a 3 day weekend? Why?

Bananas

Aeroplanes

Should students have homework?

What do you think about pay inequality?

Who is better? Male or female? Why?

How could we fix poverty in the world?

What would you do with $1 million?

Favourite musician/actor or a specific famous person- Justin Bieber, Taylor Swift

👟 FAST FINISHERS

Word in a word

Choose a word then students need to find smaller words within it. Use unit words or new words to expand vocabulary. E.g., accommodation, intimately, delegation, misbranded, disambiguation, distractedly.

My House

List 5 rooms in your house then rank them in order of importance. Write a sentence next to each room explaining why you ranked them this way.

All about you

Write your name in a creative way that tells people 10 different facts about you. Use bubble writing or block writing and illustrate inside to describe yourself.

Question the Answer

Write at least 5 questions that the answer would be…monkey, aeroplane, eggs etc.

Read a book

Silently read a book.

Tell an Alien

Describe using all your senses an object or a thing to an alien. A hug, a storm, roast chicken etc.

Change a letter

Write a 4-letter word on the board then students need to change one letter at a time to create a new word. Eg. mate, cake, time, tape, coin, hint, pile, tilt, play, pink etc.

Letter Q's

Choose a letter and students find 5-10 words to answer the following:
• Starts with B   • Ends in B   • Food   • Names

Starts with	Ends with	Food	Name
baby	comb	butter	Bob
bike	tomb	banana	Betty
book	thumb	bread	Bailey
bite	numb	beans	Brian
brain	tub	beef	Brett

Back to History

Make a list of all the things you used this morning that would not have existed 100 years ago.

Would you rather…

Write up one or a few of these to choose from.

Would you rather:
• Be left at a theme park or a department store for 24 hours?
• Drive a car or a motorbike?
• Fly or be invisible?
• Go to the moon or Disneyland?
• Be the worst player in a winning team or the best player in a losing team? Why? What would you do?

Anagrams

Make new words using all the letters once.
Eg. Anagram = Nag a ram
Word suggestions
stop, pans, spare, mean, skate, plates, steal, parties, traces, meat, etc.

NOTES

I've learned that people will forget what you said, people will forget what you did, but people will never forget how you made them feel.

-Maya Angelou

LOWER PRIMARY

I have

2 apples

plus 3 apples.

How many apples do I have altogether?

1. 2+0=   6. 7+3=
2. 3+1=   7. 9+2=
3. 5-2=   8. 12-2=
4. 10+2= 9. 5+4=
5. 0+4=   10. 9-4=

Algorithms and Word Problems
(page 103 - 106)

Addition and subtraction to 20, Count on/back, +/- 1, 2, 3, Rainbow facts (sums that equal 10), Doubles, Near Doubles, Turn Arounds, etc.

• Write sums on the board or simple word problems to be answered.

• Students can draw objects to show sums.

• Use dice to call out number sums.

Mad Minute
(page 103 - left column)

Teacher writes down 10 sums and students get one minute to answer them all.

Patterns

Make a pattern with students in front of the class e.g., boy/girl, hair or eye colour, shoes, height, etc. Then get students to make a pattern using concrete materials such as unifix blocks or counters and record them in their books. Students can then make up their own patterns e.g., flower, heart, flower… or star, circle, cross, star, circle… and draw in their books.

Ordinal Numbers

Introduce ordinal numbers by having a race either outside running, or inside- crawling around, walking, hopping or rolling marbles if available. Discuss how we use ordinal numbers to show the place of something. Have them written on paper and the spectators can award each place getter. Then practise writing and matching them as numbers and words.

1 2 3 4 5 6 7 8 9 10
11 12 13 14 15 16 17 18 19 20
21 22 23 24 25 26 27 28 29 30
31 32 33 34 35 36 37 38 39 40
41 42 43 44 45 46 47 48 49 50
51 52 53 54 55 56 57 58 59 60
61 62 63 64 65 66 67 68 69 70
71 72 73 74 75 76 77 78 79 80
81 82 83 84 85 86 87 88 89 90
91 92 93 94 95 96 97 98 99 100

88

NUMERACY

More and Less

Write 3 columns on the board and label them Less, Number and More. Choose an amount to subtract or add and get students to fill in the answers.

-10	Number	+10
	15	
	26	
	33	

Fractions

Discuss whole, halves and quarters. Students draw shapes and colour in ½, ¼, ¾, etc.

Guess a Number

Teacher says "I'm thinking of a number…" eg. 5 more than 7, a multiple of 5, 4 less than 20, higher than 24 but lower than 30, with a 4 in the tens column etc.

Graphing

Ask and record students' favourite pets, ice cream flavour, food OR use students' lunch boxes, shoes, etc. You could do a physical graph on the floor as a class and then get students to record or tally amounts and draw a picture or bar graph to show the results.

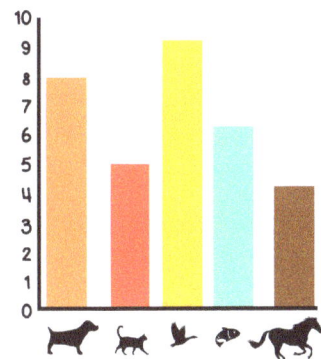

Shapes

Call out shapes and get students to draw, write their names and number of sides. If you have time, get students to draw a picture using different shapes.

Eg. A square house with a triangle roof and rectangle door, a circle sun, a semi-circle car etc.

Circle

Square

Triangle

Oval

89

NUMERACY

100's Chart Activities

There is often a hundreds chart in the room. Here are some activities you could do with one.

1	2	3	4	5	6	7	8	9	10
11	12	13	14	15	16	17	18	19	20
21	22	23	24	25	26	27	28	29	30
31	32	33	34	35	36	37	38	39	40
41	42	43	44	45	46	47	48	49	50
51	52	53	54	55	56	57	58	59	60
61	62	63	64	65	66	67	68	69	70
71	72	73	74	75	76	77	78	79	80
81	82	83	84	85	86	87	88	89	90
91	92	93	94	95	96	97	98	99	100

Counting

Counting forwards, backwards, skip counting in 2's, 5's, 10's etc.

Number Line

Use it as a number line to practice addition and subtraction.

Sum Patterns

Look for addition and subtraction patterns on the board. 4+7=11 so 14 +7=21 what would 24+7=? What pattern have you noticed? Work out some other sums using these patterns.

Missing Number

Stick on post-it notes or paper to cover a few numbers. Get the students to work out the missing number. Put a few blank numbers in a row as they improve with it. Then you can draw up some pieces of a 100's chart with missing numbers for them to answer.

Even and Odd

Discuss and show even and odd numbers. Look at the patterns on the chart. What numbers do even/odd numbers end in? Write out numbers (on the board or post-it notes etc.) and get students to decide which is odd or even.

Counting On

How many numbers from 10 to 15? How do you know? What about 10 to 25? When we count, do you include the first number, the last number, both, neither?

Up to 100

You could play this like Around the World where someone points to a number and students race to answer how many more to make 100. You could play this to 10, 20 or 50 to make it developmentally appropriate.

eg. 18 + ___ = 20

65 + ___ =100

Grid Coordinates

Using chalk or tape on the carpet or concrete, draw up a grid with coordinates (D1, B4 etc). First, get children to place objects in a given coordinate square then later, place objects in the squares and get students to identify the coordinates.

Extension
Get students to draw their own grid with coordinates and get them to draw pictures to a given coordinate.

Follow Directions

Get students to draw a picture using Positional Words eg. Draw a tree in the **middle** of the page then draw a sun in the **right hand** corner. Draw a flower **below** the tree. Draw a bee **on** the flower etc. Discuss why there were so many differences in pictures even though it was the same instructions.

Positional words

above	after	around		
			before	beginning
behind	below	beside		
			between	bottom
down	end	far		
			finish	front
in	inside	left		
			middle	near
next to	off	on		
			out	outside
over	right	start		
			through	top
under	up	upside down		

DICE ACTIVITIES

Dice activities have been designed for whole class with 2 dice. If you have a class set you can always modify the games to play in partners or groups.

These activities can also work with a pack of cards or by just giving them random numbers to use.

Adding Dice

Roll two dice (or one die twice) and add the sum of the numbers together.

3, 2	3 + 2 = 5

5, 4	54

Place Value

Roll 2 or more dice and write down the biggest number possible. Then challenge them to write the smallest number possible. If you have a lot of dice the students can challenge each other to beat the other person's number.

Roll On

Roll two dice. Put the two numbers together to make a 2-digit number then students need to count on and write the next three numbers. You can then get them to count back from the number rolled.

36	37, 38, 39...

Dice Arrays

Rolling two dice, students need to use concrete material, draw pictures or draw an array on grid paper, by multiplying the two numbers together.

NUMERACY

Roll a Rule

Give the class a starting number. Roll the dice to see what rule it will be to add and/or subtract that number 5-8 times.

13		Rule = +3	16, 19, 22, 25, 28, 31, 34, 37
40		Rule = -4	36, 32, 28, 24, 20, 16, 12, 8

Double Dice

Practise doubles by rolling one dice and getting them to double it. Then you can try rolling two dices then doubling the sum of the two numbers.

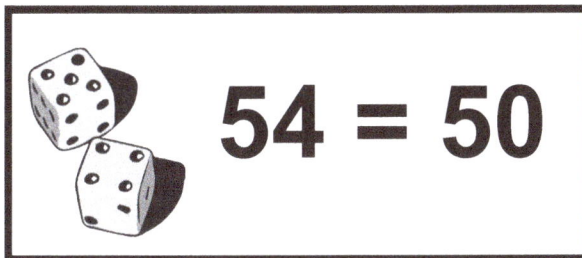

6

24

54 = 50

Roll and Round It

Roll 2 or 3 dice to create a 2 or 3-digit number then get students to round that number up or down to the closest 10 or 100.

Dice Dots

Draw or print rows of dots on a page, the amount is up to you. Next roll a dice, circle that many dots then write the number in the circle. You can play this individually, in pairs, in groups or as a whole class.

93

NUMERACY

Roll a Monster

Students draw a monster's body then they need to keep adding features for each number rolled.

add one mouth	add one eye	add one arm	add one leg	add one horn	add one spot

Playground Designer

Design a playground. Draw or write what would be in your playground.

Money, money, money!

Write down all the different coins and notes from lowest to highest value. Then write down the different coins and notes to make a set amount. Eg. $1.75, $5.30, $12.65 etc.

Impossible   Unlikely   Possible   Most Likely   Definitely

Scenario Examples

It will rain today.

February will come after January.

You will go out for dinner tonight.

It will snow on the weekend.

Tuesday will come before Monday.

Mum will pick you up from school.

You will have vegetables for dinner tonight.

You will get a hover board for your birthday.

Language of Chance

Draw a line on the board and label with Impossible, Unlikely, Possible, Most Likely and Definitely. Give students different scenarios and they choose where they fall on the line. Students then come up with 3 different scenarios that would be Impossible, Unlikely and Definitely.

Time

- Revise the days of the week, months of the year or the seasons.
  - You can ask students to write them out, arrange them in order, or work out what is missing.
  - Discuss what things you do on a certain day/month/season eg. Music on Mondays, Christmas in December, swimming in Summer, etc.

- Discuss time periods such as second, minute, hour, day, week, month, year.
  - Explain their equivalents.
  - Work out what you can do in a certain time frame eg. It takes about 1 second to clap, 1 minute to brush your teeth, 1 hour to bake a cake, 1 day at school etc.
  - Play Guess 1 Minute on page 151 to gauge an understanding of how long 1 minute is.

- Look at analogue and digital times.
  - Discuss o'clock times, half past then quarter past and quarter to depending on their ability.
  - Students could match digital with analogue, fill in the correct time or verbally tell the time.

FAST FINISHERS

0, 5, 10, 15...100

0-100

Write out your numbers 0-100. Then write in 2's, 5's, 10's to 100.

Sums

Write out rainbow facts, doubles or near doubles.

Write the Question

Write a number story for an answer. Eg. The answer is- 6 lollipops, 9 cars, 20 monkeys etc.
I had 11 lollipops and gave 5 to my friends. How many are left?

Architect Activity

Draw a plan of your bedroom/house/classroom.

Spot a shape

How many circles, triangles, squares, rectangles and other shapes can you see in the classroom?

Months

Write out the months of the year in order. Draw pictures next to each (sun, leaf, snowman, flower) to show the seasons. Write down how many days are in each month.

UPPER PRIMARY

Algorithms and Word Problems
(page 103-106)

Addition and subtraction with and without borrowing using 100's up to 100,000's using multiplication, division and fraction equivalents.

•Write sums or word problems on the board for students to answer

Maths Bingo

Students fold a piece of paper to create 16 sections, and then write a number in each square. Give them a focus/number range e.g., 8 times tables, numbers from 50-100, equivalent fractions, etc. Teacher calls out and records age-appropriate sums and students mark off their numbers with counters if their answers match. The first student to have a complete line calls out Bingo.

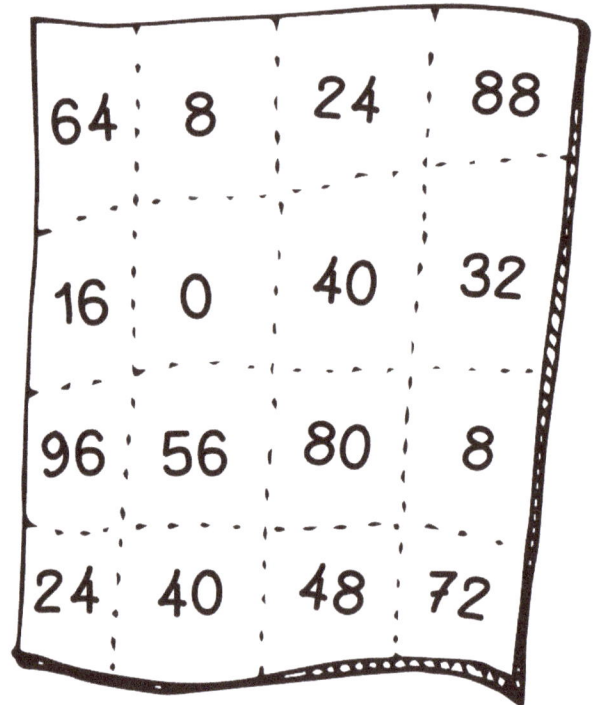

Robot Maths

Students draw a robot on grid paper then calculate the perimeter and area.

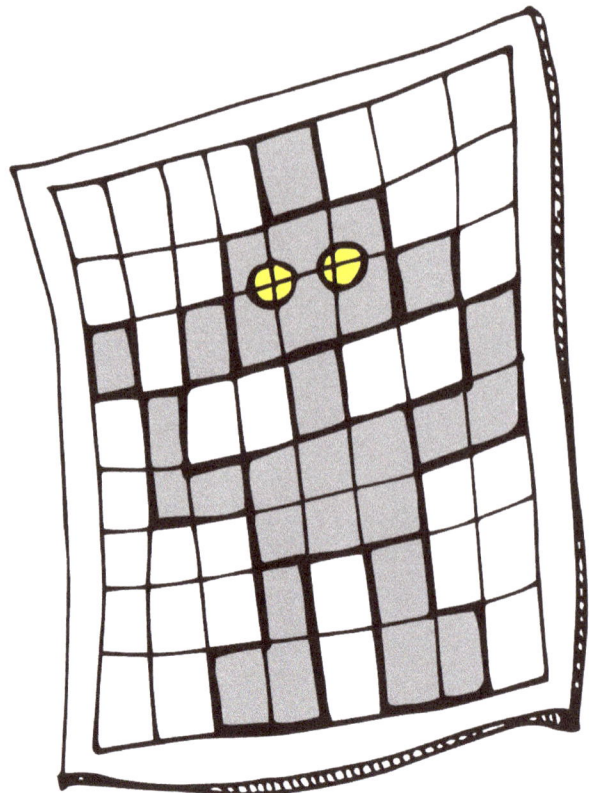

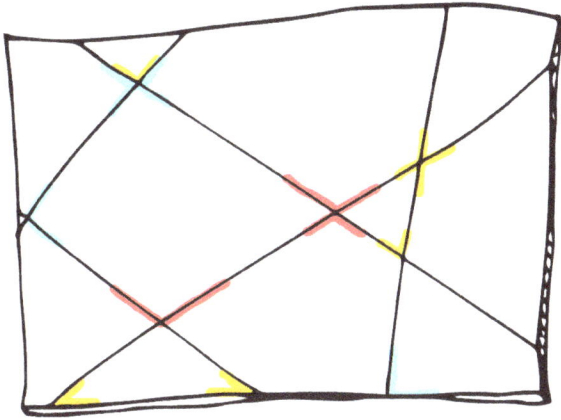

Angle Art

Students do random folds on a piece of paper, they then trace over the lines using a pencil and ruler. Discuss acute, obtuse and right angles and identify each by tracing with a specific colour. They could also measure angles with a protractor or colour in each different shape.

1. 2+0=
2. 3+1=
3. 5-2=
4. 10+2=
5. 0+4=
6. 7+3=
7. 9+2=
8. 12-2=
9. 5+4=
10. 9-4=

Mad Minute
(page 103 - left column)

Teacher writes down 10 sums and students get one minute to answer them all.

7:00 am	Wake up
7:20 am	Breakfast
8:00 am	Go to school
9:00 am	Start school
3:00 pm	Finish school
3:30pm	Homework
4:00pm	Play
6:00pm	Dinner
8:00pm	Bedtime

Daily Schedule

Write down all the things you do in a day and at what time. What takes you the longest/shortest amount of time? How long do you sleep? What are you doing at 6:30 pm?

Rounding

Rounding numbers to the nearest 10's, 100's, 1 000's, 10 000's and 100 000's.

Number	10's	100's	1 000's	10 000's	100 000's
37 525	37 530	37 500	38 000	40 000	---
134 789	134 790	134 800	135 000	130 000	100 000
528 124	528 120	528 100	528 000	530 000	500 000

NUMERACY

DICE ACTIVITIES

Dice activities have been designed for whole class with 2 dice. If you have a class set you can always modify the games to play in partners or groups.

These activities can also work with a pack of cards or by just giving them random numbers to use.

Game of Greed

Students set up their paper in columns as shown. Each column is a new game. Everyone is standing and records the product of two dice that are rolled. They can choose to sit down and 'bank' their totals at any stage, but if they do they can not stand up again. If a 1 is rolled, the game ends and the students still standing lose all their points for that round. If it lands on double 1 then they lose all their points for all the previous games too. Winner has the highest total for the games played. A great game of risk, chance and greed!

G	R	E	E	D
15	4	10	18	16
6	9	25	9	20
30	36	6	12	4
4	20	—	36	9
24	24	41	8	10
—	8		6	12
79	18		9	—
	8		24	71
	20		—	
	—		164	
	147			

Greedy Pig

Choose a number on the dice to be the Greedy Pig number. The teacher or students roll the dice continually, recording each number on the board until the Greedy Pig number is rolled. Students begin the game standing, and sit down once they want to 'bank' their total. The aim is to sit down before the Greedy Pig number comes up. Students copy down each number as they go and add up their total at the end. You can change the number and discuss the Language of Chance.

④

6 1 2 1 3 4 3 3 1
5 3 5 6 2 2 1 4

Order of Operations

Using a sum layout like the one beside, roll the dice and use the numbers to create the sum then work out the answer.

Layout
_ _ + (___ + ___) =
_ _ + (___ - ___) =
(___ x ___) + __ =
_ + _ + (__ - __) =

Examples
32 + (5 + 4) = 41
41 + (6 - 3) = 44
(6 x 5) + 3 = 33
3 + 2 +(6 - 1) = 10

NUMERACY

Bankrupt	$2	$5	$10	$20	$50

Dollar Dice

Each number has a monetary value. Using the rules of Greedy Pig, students add up money as it is rolled then they need to sit down when they want to "bank" their money. Choose money values according to ability.

Or, if you have a class set of dice, students can race each other taking turns to roll a die to reach a certain dollar value.

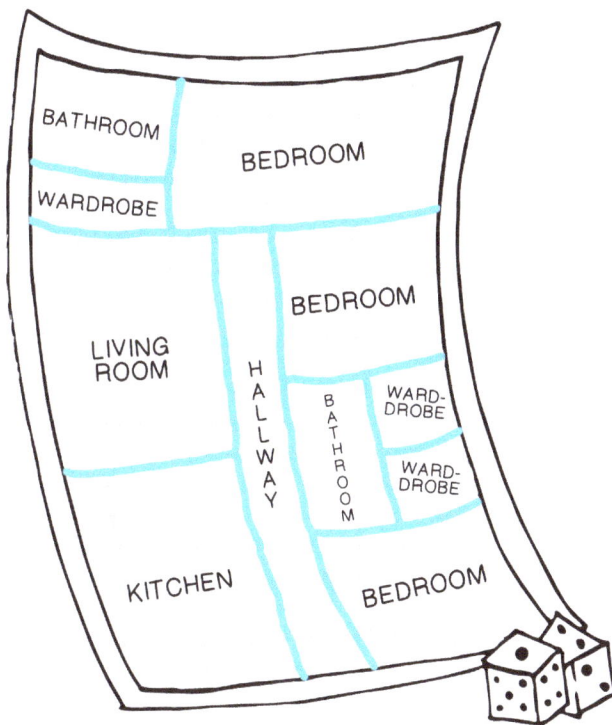

Design a House Dice Game

Two dice are rolled and these numbers become the perimeter of a rectangle or square. Draw the dimensions using grid squares then students then need to find the area of the shape. On the next roll, extend on the shape to create another room on the house design and find the area of that room. They can then find the total area of the house plan.

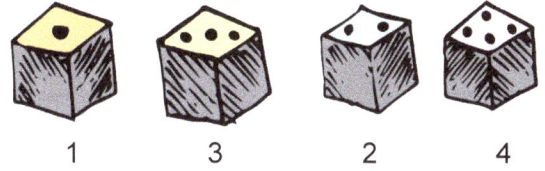

$$\tfrac{1}{3} + \tfrac{2}{4} = \tfrac{4}{12} + \tfrac{6}{12} = \tfrac{10}{12} = \tfrac{5}{6}$$

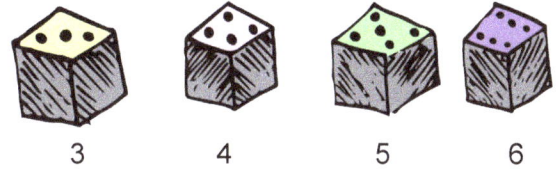

$$\tfrac{3}{4} + \tfrac{5}{6} = \tfrac{18}{24} + \tfrac{20}{24} = \tfrac{38}{24} = 1\,\tfrac{14}{24} \text{ or } 1\,\tfrac{7}{12}$$

Fraction Sums

Roll two dice and use the smaller number as the numerator (top number) and the larger number as the denominator (bottom number) or in any order for higher ability students. Roll them again to get another fraction then either add, subtract, multiply or divide the fractions depending on their ability.

Remind them that they need a common denominator. To do this, multiply the denominators together then cross multiply. So, multiply the first numerator with the second denominator. Then multiply the second numerator with the first denominator. They can then simplify the fraction once they have their answer.

Fraction Order

Roll two dice and use the numbers to create a fraction. Repeat 3 or more times, then get students to put the fractions in order of smallest to largest then largest to smallest.

Improper Fraction

Roll three dice (or one die three times) to create an improper fraction then get students to simplify it. Eg. If 3, 4, 6 is rolled some possible answers could be 34/6 = 5 4/6 or 43/6 = 7 1/6 or 64/3 = 21 1/3

99

NUMERACY

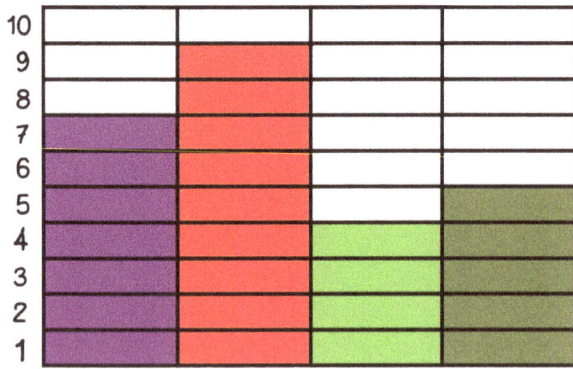

Graphing

Ask and record students' favourite pets, ice cream flavour, food OR use students' lunch boxes, shoes, etc. You could do a physical graph on the floor as a class and then get students to draw a picture or bar graph to show the results. Draw tally marks, put results into a table and then draw the graph.

Then ask students questions such as-
What was the most/least popular?
How many _____ were there?
How many _____ and _____ are there in total?
How many more _____ than _____?

Around the world

One student stands behind another student who is sitting at their desk. Teacher asks them a sum and the first student to answer correctly progresses to the next desk.

Name Angles

Students write their names using straight lines only, then measure the angles using their protractor.

Follow Directions
(List of positional words on Page 91)

Get students to draw a picture using positional language eg. draw 2 lines to make 4 quadrants. In the **top right hand** quadrant, draw a tree. In the **bottom left hand** quadrant, draw an orange sun. In the bottom right hand quadrant find the **top right hand** corner and write your initials/age/number of people in your family. Below that draw a purple star etc.

Note – As you go, draw it yourself to use as an example to compare with the students at the end.

NUMERACY

Calculator words

Students add up the sums on their calculator then they turn the calculator upside down which will reveal a word to answer the clue. Eg. 317 turned upside down is LIE

1. 7 152 – 47 = dirt (SOIL)
2. 400 – 83 = tell no truth (LIE)
3. 115 469 x 5 = peanut cases (SHELL)
4. 8 000 – 265 = trade (SELL)
5. 3 838 ÷ 101= exist   (BE)
6. 57 000 + 738 = these ring (BELLS)
7. 461 000 + 375 = Santa's transport (SLEIGH)
8. 2 689 403 x 2 = turkey sound (GOBBLES)
9. 269 038 + 269 038 = light bulbs (GLOBES)
10. 1 214 – 607 = tree trunk (LOG)
11. 133 877 x 4 = people in charge (BOSSES)
12. 213 803 x 25 = water sound (SLOSHES)
13. 8 834 x 4 = honking birds (GEESE)
14. 13 426 x 4 = openings (HOLES)
15. 7 502 ÷ 2 = island (ISLE)
16. 11 669 x 3 = not tight (LOOSE)
17. 1 772 569 x 3 = sweets (LOLLIES)
18. 14 429 x 4 = used by fish (GILLS)
19. 1 327 x 40 = wind instrument (OBOES)
20. 9 135 ÷ 3 = footwear (SHOE)
21. 5 000+ 600+ 60+ 3 = laid by hens (EGGS)
22. 0.3 x 2 = leave (GO)
23. 0.47 x 1.5 = alone (SOLO)
24. 0.4 x 0.2 = scare word (BOO)

Guess the Number

3 students out the front of the class guessing the number. Teacher picks a number (can be one number or one number each) and students need to guess the number without just saying only numbers. Students should ask questions such as, is it odd, does it have x numbers, is it higher than, is it a multiple of 5, is the number in the thousands column bigger than the ones column? The aim is to ask the least amount of questions to guess the number.

542

12,240

5,983

FAST FINISHERS

Write the Question

Write a number story for an answer eg. The answer is... 16 marbles, 24 lollipops, 6 cars, 9 monkeys, 8 eggs, 60 balloons etc. Students rewarded for most challenging question.

Architect Activity

Draw a bird's eye view picture of your bedroom/house/classroom.

Times Tables

Write out your times tables.

I'm rich!

You are given $500,000. What would you spend it on? How would you divide your money?

1247
2147
2417
4172
7142

4 digit Numbers

Write down 4 digits. Write down all the different numbers you can make with all 4 digits and then put them in ascending/decending order.

NUMERACY

MATH ALGORITHMS

Lower Years			
1. 4 + 1 =	5	11. 3 + 3 =	6
2. 2 + 2 =	4	12. 5 + 3 =	8
3. 6 + 4 =	10	13. How many sides in an octagon?	8
4. 5 + 0 =	5	14. 7 + __ = 10	3
5. 9 - 1 =	8	15. What is the month after May?	June
6. 14 + 2 =	16	16. 15 + 3 =	18
7. 10 + 10 =	20	17. 19 + 0 =	19
8. 13 + 2 =	15	18. What number comes before 16?	15
9. 12 - 2 =	10	19. How many days are in a week?	7
10. 17 - 3 =	14	20. 15 - 4 =	11

Middle Years			
1. 15 + 4 =	19	11. 233 + 43 =	276
2. 22 - 2 =	20	12. 5 x 3 =	15
3. 11 + 3 =	14	13. How many sides in a pentagon?	5
4. 29 - 1 =	28	14. 550 + 150 =	700
5. 15 + 10 =	25	15. How many days in July?	31
6. 3 x 0 =	0	16. 100 + 40 + 6 =	146
7. 20 + 20 =	40	17. 26 + ___ = 36	10
8. 100 + 13 =	113	18. 20 x 2 =	40
9. 11 x 5 =	55	19. How many days in a year?	365
10. 4 x 3 =	12	20. 8 x 5 =	40

Upper Years			
1. 34 + 11 =	45	11. 120 x 7 =	840
2. 12 x 3 =	36	12. 4055 + 9275 =	13330
3. 17 + 13 =	30	13. How many sides in a hexagon?	6
4. 54 + 4 =	58	14. 140 + ___ = 230	90
5. 199 + 2 =	201	15. How many months have 30 days?	4
6. 144 - 2 =	142	16. 132 ÷ 11 =	12
7. 12 x 5 =	60	17. 58 x 17 =	969
8. 9 x 6 =	54	18. 10000 + 5000 + 400 + 2 =	15 402
9. 90 - 11 =	79	19. How many hours in 3 days?	72
10. 45 ÷ 5 =	9	20. 468 ÷ 9 =	52

WORD PROBLEMS

Lower Years

There were 5 hippos in the water and 2 more came along. How many hippos were there altogether?

5 + 2 = 7 hippos

There were 8 mangoes on a tree and 2 fell off. How many mangoes are left on the tree?

8 - 2 = 6 mangoes

There were 5 boys in the group and 5 girls. How many children were there altogether?

5 + 5 = 10 children

11 children were invited to my party but 2 can't come. How many children are still coming?

11 - 2 = 9 children

If there are 13 red marbles and 4 blue marbles, how many marbles are there in total?

13 + 4 = 17 marbles

Cleo had 14 cupcakes for her birthday and there were only 10 people. How many cupcakes were leftover?

14 - 10 = 4 cupcakes

There are two red cars in the driveway. How many wheels are there altogether?

4 + 4 = 8 or 2 x 4 = 8 wheels

There are 6 blueberries to share between 3 children. How many blueberries would each child get?

6 ÷ 3 = 2 blueberries

There were 3 paddocks with 4 cows in each. How many cows are there in total?

4 + 4 + 4 = 12 or 3 x 4 = 12 cows

There are 14 people that need to be divided equally into 2 teams.
How many people should there be in each team?

14 ÷ 2 = 7 people

Eva has 5 stickers, Koa has 3 and Lianie has 7. How many stickers are there altogether?

5 + 3 + 7 = 15 stickers

Charlotte had 17 grapes. Poppy took 2 grapes away and Georgie took 4. How many grapes does Charlotte have left?

17 - 2 - 4 = 11 grapes

NUMERACY

Middle Years

There are 22 girls and 53 boys in the hall. How many girls and boys are in the hall all together? **22 + 53 = 75 girls and boys**	There are 25 more tigers than lions in the zoo. There are 16 lions. How many tigers are there? **16 + 25 = 41 tigers**
Oliver has 54 red blocks and 40 green blocks. How many blocks does Oliver have altogether? **54 + 40 = 94 blocks**	Matilda has 47 stickers and Amelia has 28 stickers. How many more stickers does Matilda have than Amelia? **47 - 28 = 19 stickers**
Dusty has 79 action figures and Maxie has 43 action figures. How many more action figures does Dusty have than Maxie? **79 - 43 = 36 action figures**	There are 142 ants and 118 bugs in the garden. How many fewer bugs are there than ants? **142 - 118 = 24 bugs**
Sari has 60 ribbons and Delilah has 19 ribbons. How many more ribbons does Sari have than Delilah? **60 - 19 = 41 ribbons**	In the quilt, there are 8 fabric squares in each row and there are 5 rows. How many fabric squares are there all together? **8 x 5 = 40 fabric squares**
Byron had 15 balloons to put onto 3 tables for her birthday party. How many balloons are on each table? **15 ÷ 3 = 5 balloons**	Each shelf in the library has 9 books. If there are 90 books all together, how many shelves are there? **90 ÷ 9 = 10 shelves**
Cayden put 32 cookies on trays. If there were 8 trays and he put the same number of cookies on each tray, how many cookies did he put on each tray? **32 ÷ 8 = 4 cookies**	There were 34 planes at the airport. 19 planes landed and 15 more took off. How many planes are there now at the airport? **34 +19 = 53** **53 - 15 = 38 planes**

Upper Years

There are 278 snakes, 387 spiders, 142 lizards and 49 crocodiles in the wildlife park. How many reptiles are in the park? 278 + 142 + 49 = 469 reptiles	There are 1578 students in the school. If 649 are in the Senior school, how many students are in the Junior school? 1578 - 649 = 929 students
Neve has 74 stickers. She gave 4 stickers each to 7 friends. How many stickers are left over? 4 x 7 = 28 74 - 28 = 46 stickers	There are 56 zebras that need to be put into 8 fields. How many zebras will be in each field? 56 ÷ 8 = 7 zebras
Bonnie went shopping and bought 6 pairs of shoes for $156 each. How much did she spend in total? $156 x 6 = $936	The perimeter of a regular pentagon is 125cm. How long is each side? 125 ÷ 5 = 25cm
7 packets of crackers have 19 in them while 4 packets have 22 each. How many crackers are there altogether? 7 x 19 = 133 4 x 22 = 88 133 + 88 = 221 crackers	8 cats have 9 kittens each. How many felines are there altogether? 8 x 9 = 72 kittens + 8 cats = 80 felines
Noah watches 4 footy matches every weekend and one extra match every fortnight on a Wednesday. The football season goes for 18 weeks. How many matches does he watch all season? 4 x 18 = 72 (weekends) 18 ÷ 2 = 9 (fortnights) 72 + 9 = 81 matches	Van needs $148 to buy a new bike. He got $45 for his birthday and $37 for doing chores. How much more money does he need? 45 + 37= $82 148 - 82 = $66
Travis earns $17 per hour. He worked 5 hours on Monday, 6 hours on Tuesday, 4 hours on Wednesday, 8 hours on Thursday, and 9 hours on Friday. How much did he earn all week? Total hrs worked = 5 + 6 + 4 + 8 + 9 = 32 $17 x 32 =$544	Ande bought two ice creams for $3.60 each, three sandwiches for $6.70 each, three bottles of water for $2.95 each and seven apples for $0.75 each. How much change does she get from $50? Total for food $3.60 x 2 = $7.20 $6.70 x 3 = $20.10 $2.95 x 3 = $ 8.85 $0.75 x 7 = $5.25 Total = $41.40 Change = $50 - $41.40 = $8.60

NOTES

A good teacher can inspire hope, ignite the imagination and instil a love of learning.

-**Brad Henry**

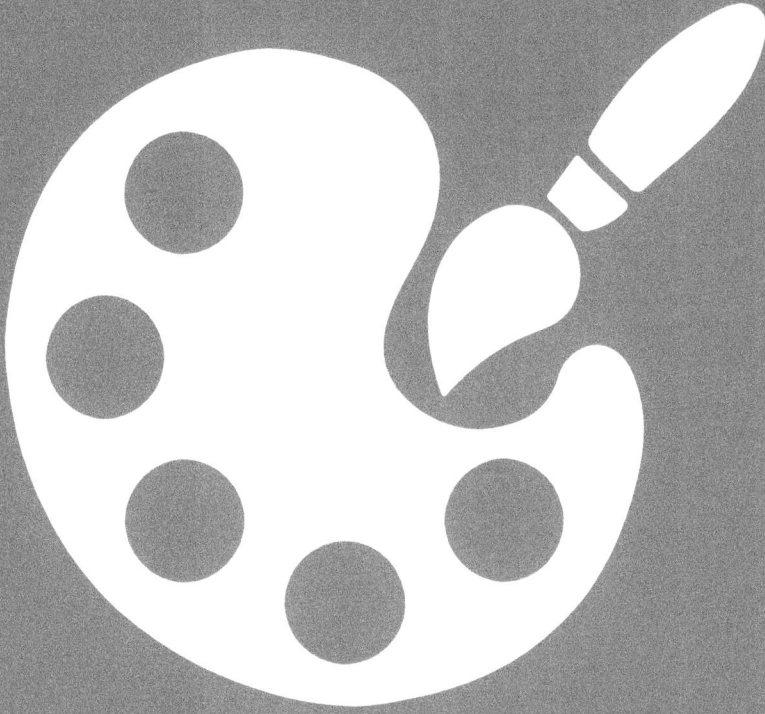

Art

LOWER PRIMARY

Story Drawing

From a book familiar to the class, draw one of the characters, draw a setting, or draw both. Either the teacher directs students step by step, or students draw their own interpretation.

Psychedelic Squiggles

Students draw squiggly, loopy lines all over a page in black marker. Then, using crayons or pencils, students will shade approximately 1 cm perpendicular to the line in various colours and continue to colour until the page is full.

Name Tag

Get students to design a desk tag to help you
learn their names.

Draw a Lion

Using shapes and lines, guide the students step-by-step to create this lion.

Newspaper Cats

Create a cat out of cut out newspaper. It will need a rounded head, a semi-oval body and triangular ears made from newspaper. Then, on plain paper they can draw, colour and cut out the eyes, whiskers and collar then glue them on the cat and glue onto plain or coloured paper.

You could also make a dog, rabbit or other basic animal as an alternative.

ART

UPPER PRIMARY

Zentangle Hands

Trace your hand, break it up into about 10 sections then fill with different doodles to create your Zentangle designs.

Magazine Symmetry

Using a large face or picture from a magazine, cut it in half, glue onto a blank piece of paper and then draw the other half of the picture using a lead pencil. Students draw it in real life or fantasy.

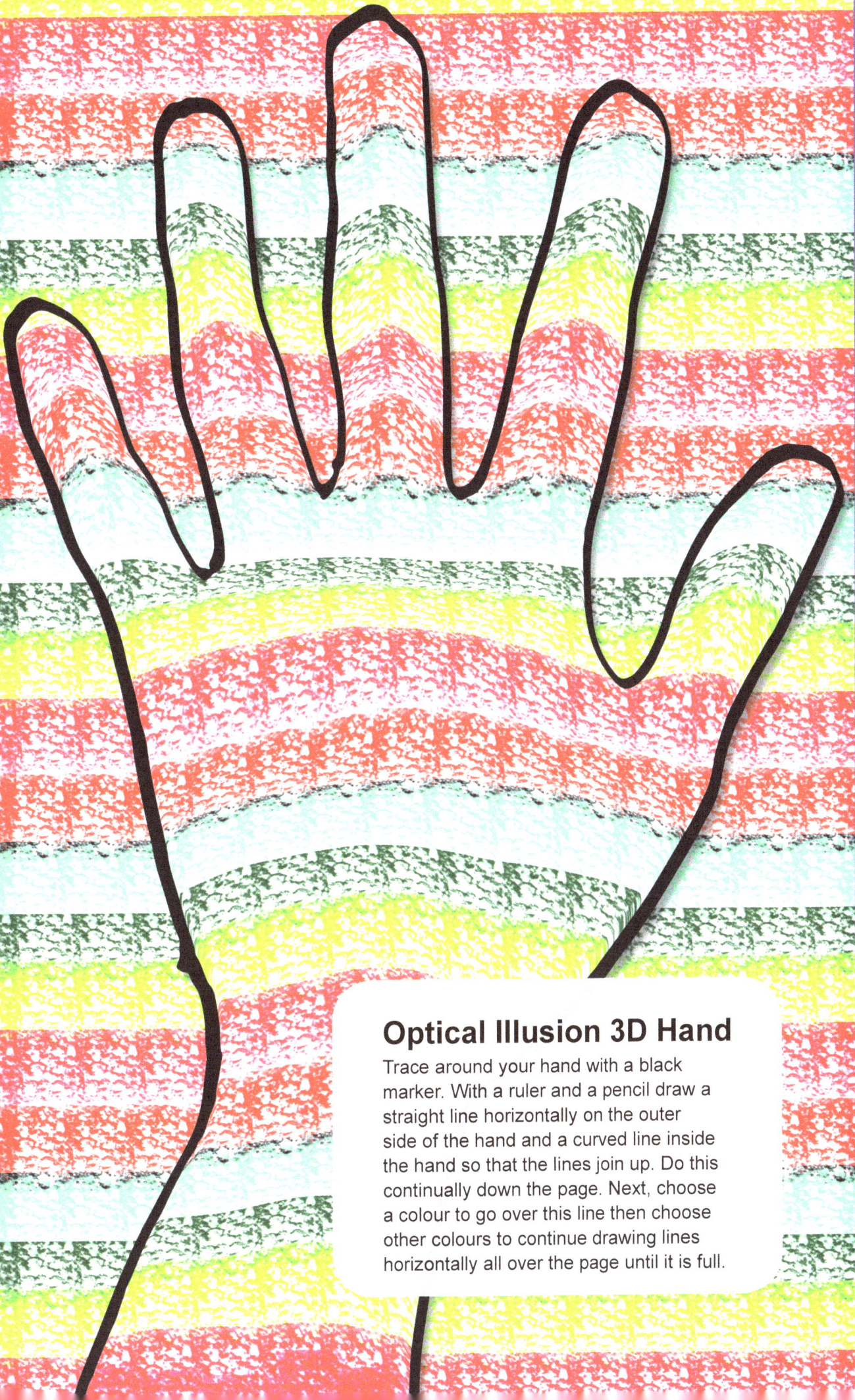

Optical Illusion 3D Hand

Trace around your hand with a black marker. With a ruler and a pencil draw a straight line horizontally on the outer side of the hand and a curved line inside the hand so that the lines join up. Do this continually down the page. Next, choose a colour to go over this line then choose other colours to continue drawing lines horizontally all over the page until it is full.

ART

One Point Perspective

Get students to draw a landscape picture such as a road or train track heading to the mountains with trees, power poles or a fence running along by it. Explain the need to keep the horizontal and vertical lines as straight as possible but everything will angle towards a "Vanishing Point". Draw faint lines that angle back to the "Vanishing Point" to keep everything aligned to create the illusion of distance.

Step 1. Determine the horizon and vanishing point of your drawing.

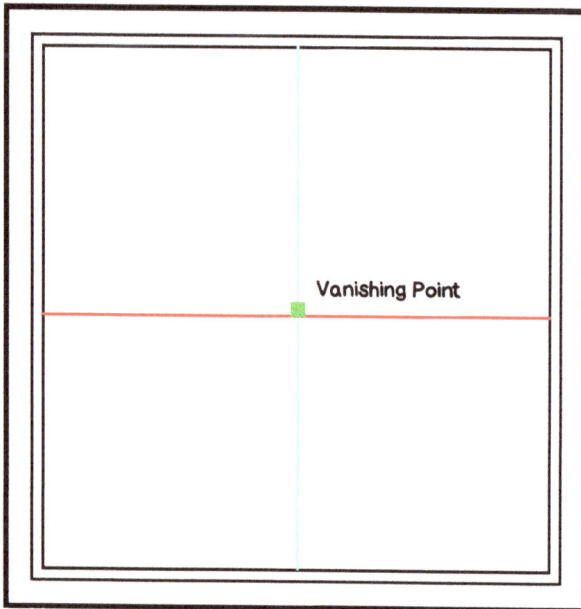

Vanishing Point

Step 2. Start sketching the main objects.

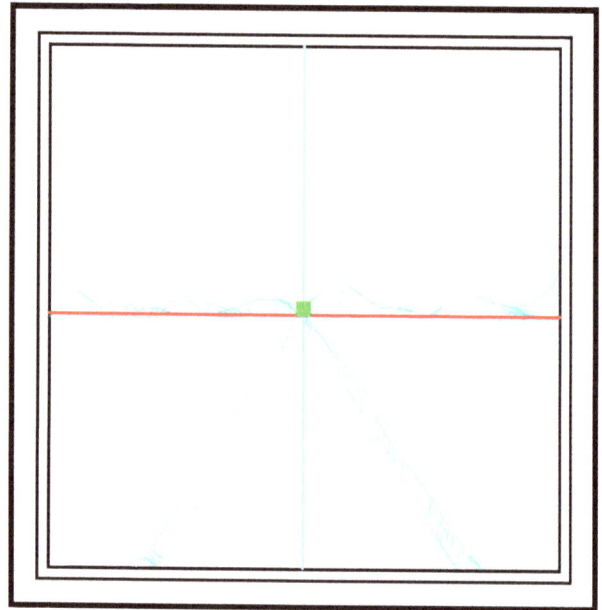

Step 3. Add details and furnish your sketch with a marker or pen.

Step 4. Finish your drawing by erasing the imaginary lines and vanishing point.

ART

Eye Reflection

Students are to draw an eye and in the pupil will be a reflection of somewhere they would love to be. This could be the beach, mountains, football field, bike track etc.

Line and Colour

Explore line and colour with this simple but effective side profile piece. Start with a wavy line down the centre of the page. Draw a profile of a face then fill with colour blocks. Finish off drawing straight vertical and horizontal lines for contrasting effect.

LOWER PRIMARY and
UPPER PRIMARY

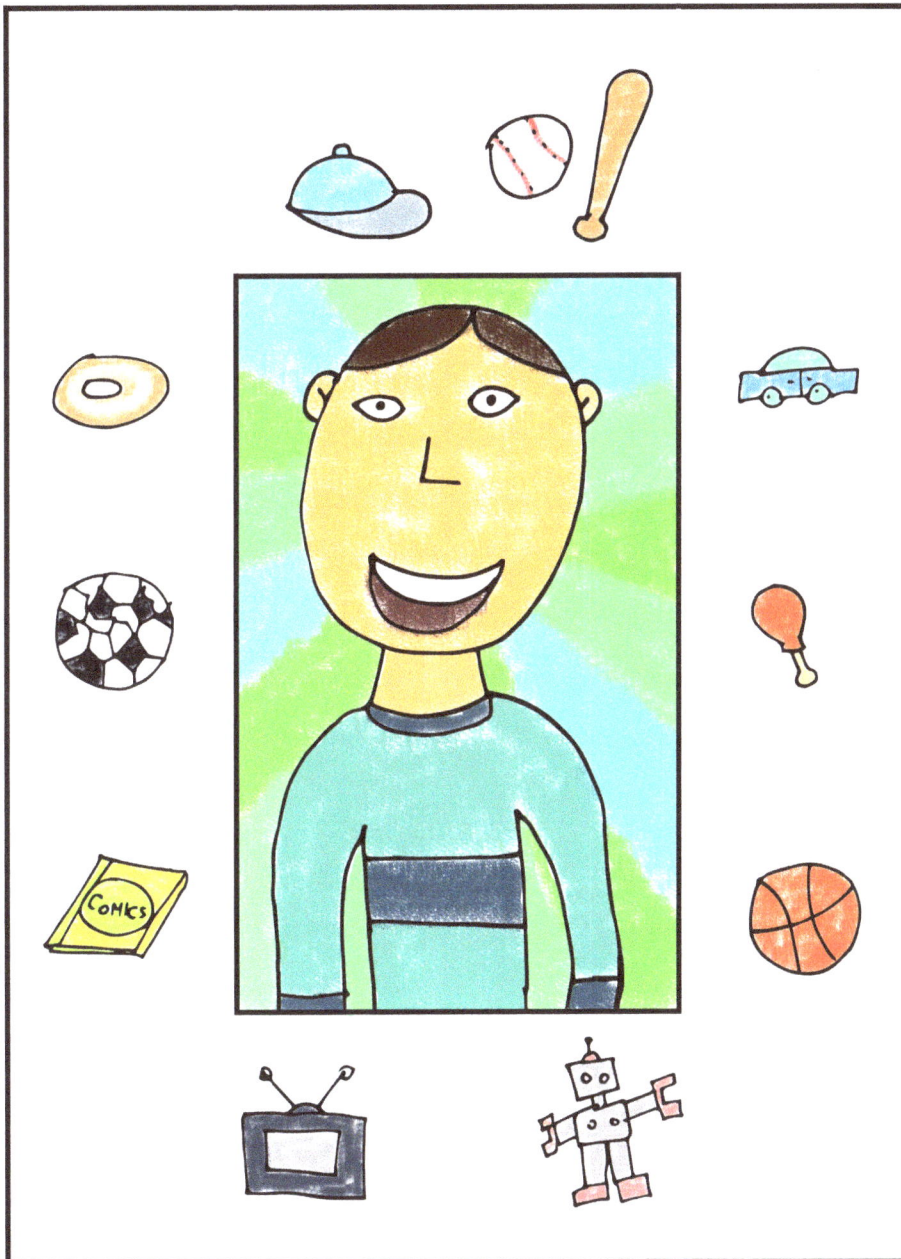

Self Portrait

Using crayons or pencils, students draw a portrait of themselves. Include a border that has things they love in it e.g., sports, food, music, etc.

ART

Magazine Tearing

Tear magazines to decorate a picture/shape. Students need to find similar colours eg. draw a tree and find greens and browns to glue on.

Textured Landscapes

Students draw a simple landscape picture and
fill it in using different colours and patterns.

ART

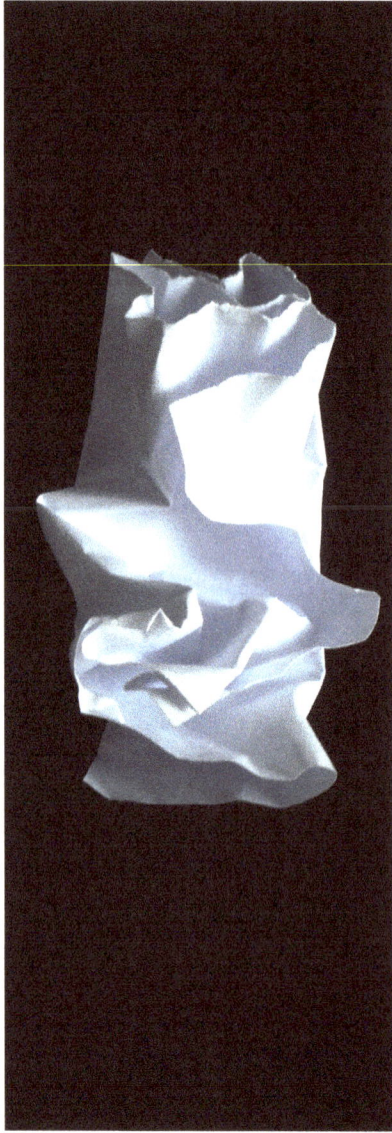

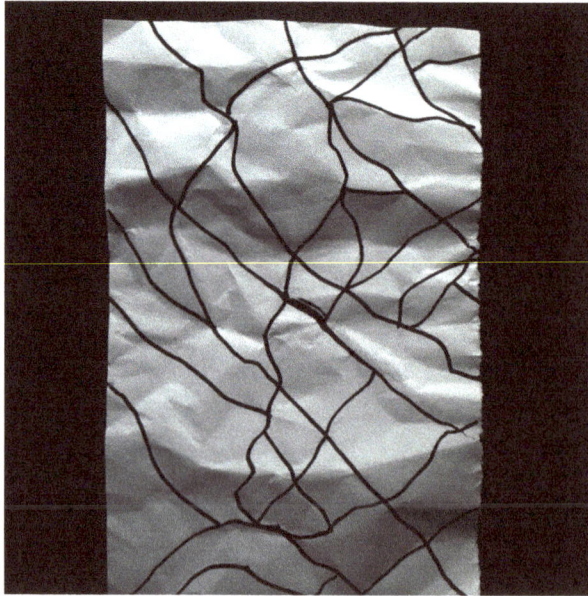

Crumpled Paper Art

Students crumple up a piece of paper and then open it up and flatten it out. Using a black marker or pencil, draw the lines that it has made. Colour in each section with a different colour pencil or crayon.

You can turn this activity into a behaviour discussion called Words Do Hurt. Students scrunch the paper for every time someone has said something hurtful. When unfolding the paper discuss that, although the paper is intact, it has marks left on it. Explain that words have the same effect on us.

NOTES

ART

There are no secrets to success. It is the result of preparation, hard work and learning from failure.

-Colin Powell

Drama and Music

LOWER PRIMARY

Doggy, Doggy, Where's Your Bone?

Students sit in a large circle. The teacher chooses a student to be the 'doggy' and to close their eyes in the middle of the circle. The teacher gives an item (the bone) to one of the students sitting in the circle to hide behind their back.

The class sings "Doggy, doggy where's your bone, somebody stole it from your home. Guess who, maybe you? Wake up doggy, find your bone."

The 'doggy' in the middle of the circle gets 3 guesses at who is hiding the 'bone' behind their back.

Name Syllables

Sitting in a circle, students count and clap out the syllables in your name. This is a great way to learn students' names.

Al-ex-an-der

Musical Freeze

Play music and students freeze when the music stops.

DRAMA AND MUSIC

Bean Game

Students do the actions of each bean when the teacher calls them out. Choose some or all of these.

Jelly bean	wobbling	Butter Bean	slide around on your bottom
Jumping bean	jump on the spot	Full of Beans	dance around energetically
Runner bean	run on the spot	Coffee bean	cough madly
Chili bean	shiver and shake	Tinned beans	get into small groups
Frozen bean	freeze	Bean Casserole	students all join hands
Broad bean	giant steps around the room	Beanstalk	crouch down and grow up to the sky
Baked bean	sunbake on the floor	Magic Bean	wave a wand
String bean	arms straight up in the air as thin as string	Bean bag	one student sits on the floor and a partner sits on their lap

Pick the Missing Object

Students sit in a large circle. Have different objects in the middle of the circle and cover with a towel/ jumper. While students cover their eyes, remove an object. Uncover the remaining objects and students will then guess what object is missing.

UPPER PRIMARY

Postcards

Students are put into groups and are then given a topic to create a freeze frame picture e.g,. a wedding, beach holiday, Australia, America, Eiffel Tower, Sydney Harbour Bridge, Uluru, Olympic rowing team, Naplan, school disco.

Body Spelling

Students use their bodies to spell out given words.

Get in Order

Without talking, students must get in order of height, birthday months, alphabetical order, etc.

Wink Murder

One student is the 'detective' and needs to leave the room. Students sit in a circle and the teacher chooses a 'murderer.' When the detective returns, the murderer must discreetly wink at students in the circle to kill them. Students can then die (as dramatically as they like) and the detective gets 3 guesses to work out who the murderer is.

Two Truths and a Lie

Students take it in turns to tell the class two truthful things about themselves and one lie. The class needs to pick the lie.

DRAMA AND MUSIC

LOWER PRIMARY and UPPER PRIMARY

Nursery Rhyme Mix-up

In groups or individually, students perform a nursery rhyme in different formats. Have students draw different topics out of a hat.

Twinkle, Twinkle, Little Star	Robot voice
Baa Baa Black Sheep	Rap
Row, Row, Row your Boat	Opera
Happy Birthday	Foreign Accent
Incy Wincy Spider	Deep Voice
Humpty Dumpty	Helium Voice
I'm a Little Teapot	With a blocked nose
Jack and Jill	Baby voice

Musical Heads

Similar to Celebrity Heads, however the students need to guess the musical instrument. Students ask questions such as – "Am I a wind/string/brass instrument?" "Would I be played in a rock band/orchestra?"

Musical Maze

A maze is made up using books, chairs, jumpers, hats, etc. Directions will be allocated sounds e.g., left = clap, right = click, forward = la, backward = stomp, stop = bang. The whole class needs to safely direct the student through the maze.

Storm Musical

Using body parts only, students are to create a storm musical. They will start with the pitter patter of rain drops, moving on to a light shower and progress to a heavy downpour. Choose some students to add in the howling wind and claps of thunder. Once they have reached the crescendo of the storm, get students to quiet down to the pitter patter and then stop.

Found Sound

Students explore the room and find something they can use to make a sound. They will share their Found Sound and can vote on the most original sound.

Clusters

Give students an instruction (walk backwards, crawl, hop, tiptoe, stomp, jump, etc.), call out a number and the students need to get into groups of this amount. It is a good way to get students into groups for a follow-up activity.

DRAMA AND MUSIC

Charades

Students act out a movie, TV show or book; breaking up the title into words and acting out each word without speaking.

Spider Web Tangle

Students hold hands in a circle, then mix up without breaking the chain. They then need to untangle themselves without letting go.

Minute Mime

Give students an action to act out silently and the class can guess what it is e.g., snake, running a race, riding a scooter, playing basketball, playing the guitar, brushing your teeth.

Lion **(stalking and attacking its prey)**	Watching television **(something scary comes on)**
Brushing your hair **(that is really knotty)**	Riding a bike **(and the chain keeps falling off)**
Surfing **(and you spot a shark)**	Walking the dog **(and it stops to do a poo)**
Flying a kite **(on a very windy day)**	Doing Karate **(breaking a board)**
Playing the drums **(in a rock band)**	Playing soccer **(scoring a goal)**
Riding a horse **(and it bucks you off)**	Eating an ice cream **(and it is melting quickly)**
Putting on glasses **(and you clean them as they are dirty)**	Grocery shopping **(and your trolley is overflowing with food)**
Washing your hair **(and you get shampoo in your eyes)**	Getting dressed **(and you realise your shirt is inside out)**

DRAMA AND MUSIC

NOTES

NOTES

DRAMA AND MUSIC

2 Truths   and a Lie

Three students stand up the front of the class. They are to say three sentences about their family, self description or pets. One of the sentences must be a lie and the class needs work out what they said and who was lying.

Examples:

I have one brother.

I have two sisters.

I have three sisters.

Directional Maze

 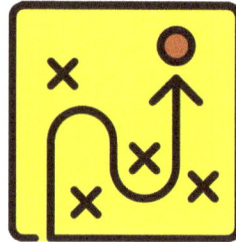 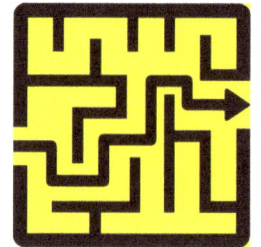

Create a maze around the classroom and using directional language students are to direct each other from one side to the other.

Eg. Right two steps, stop, go straight ahead, left one step etc.

Splat!

Write up some vocabulary words randomly on the board. Students are in teams and need to race to "Splat" or touch the correct word when the teacher calls out.

Dos Cinco
Siete Diez
Uno Ocho Nueve
Cuatro Seis Tres

Pictionary

Split the class in half. Choose one student from each team to draw. Whisper a word to them both, then they have 30sec-1 min to draw it. The first team to guess correctly gets a point.

2 Step Charades

Students spread out around the classroom. The teacher calls out a foreign word and students raise their hand to answer them. If they get it correct they get to take two, standard paces in any direction. The aim is to try and tag someone to get them out and be the last student standing.

139

LOTE

Around the World

One student stands behind another student who is sitting at their desk. The teacher says a word in either English or the LOTE language and the first student to answer correctly moves on to the next desk.

NOTES

NOTES

The difference between ordinary
and extraordinary is that little extra.

-Jimmy Johnson

Games

ICE BREAKERS

Remembering names of new children every day can be hard. Little games or discussions can help you remember them faster.

Ask students their name with some extra info such as -
* Something interesting about yourself.
* A nickname.
* If you were an animal what would you be?
* An adjective that starts with the same letter as your name. Eg. Jolly Jasper.

Name Aerobics

Get students to tell you their name and do actions for each syllable of their name. The class then repeats the name and the actions.

Four Squares

Get students to rule up a page in quarters. In each quarter they will draw a picture that helps describe them. Each box will have a topic such as your family, your hobbies, favourite place to go, important things in your life, if you were an animal what would you be etc.?

Line Up

Students line themselves up in order of height, alphabetical order, birthdays, house number etc. It will start off chaotic but you will quickly see some order and organisation.

Special Artefact

Get students to grab one thing from their desk and as they introduce themselves they explain why that thing is special to them.

BRAIN BREAK

Mindful Meditation

You can access online tools or apps such as Smiling Minds or just put on some calming music and talk the class through some visualisation and relaxation.

"You are floating in a cool, freshwater pool. There is a waterfall running nearby. You can hear the sounds of birds and crickets around you. Notice how the water feels all around you. Notice how peaceful it is relaxing in the cool, shallow water. Your body is completely relaxed…"

Yoga

Yoga is a great skill for stretching, calming and promoting mindfulness and awareness of the body and breathing. Practise Downward Dog, Cat and Cow Pose, Child's Pose, Standing Tree Pose, Star Pose, Warrior Pose, Cobra (with tongue out) etc. Improvise a rocket launching into space, the sun rising, butterflies opening their wings and trees swaying side to side.

Images from Go Noodle

10 star jumps *12 jumps* *8 side steps*

4 frog jumps *1 minute running in place* *8 one foot hop*

Go Noodle

Go Noodle is a great online tool to practise movement and mindfulness. There are hundreds of activities and videos that you can access for free that help activate children's bodies and minds. www.gonoodle.com

Get moving

Call out random movements for the students to do. "10 star jumps, 5 push-ups, 7 squats, 14 sit-ups etc."

Stretching

You could choose a student or demonstrate yourself some stretches for the class to follow.

Thumb War

With a partner, students link hands and do a good old fashion thumb wrestle.

Doodle time

Give students some scrap paper to draw on for 5 minutes. Try using both hands at the same time or drawing with your less dominate hand.

Shared Drawing

A student draws for 1 minute then swaps with someone. They continue swapping either around the room or with a partner and observe how an idea evolves.

GAMES

Scissors, Paper, Rock

Teach the children the rules of this favourite hand game and how scissors beats paper, paper beats rock and rock beats scissors then get them to play with a partner.

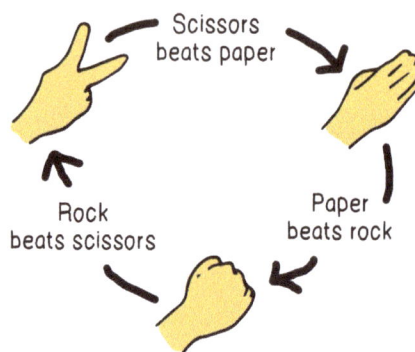

Mirror, Mirror

With a partner, get the students to face each other and get one student to lead by doing slow movements while the other person copies or "mirrors" them.

Stop! Go!

Give students actions to do (running, walking, jumping, crawling, dancing etc) then give them instructions to stop, go, slow motion, speedy, loudly, quietly etc.

Corners

Designate different corners or parts of the room as something they have been learning. Children need to choose one and move to the area. You can then call or draw from a hat one of the corners and anyone standing in that corner needs to sit down.

LOWER PRIMARY

Pizza Massage

Students sit in a circle all facing one direction so they can touch the student in front's back. Then, following the teacher's instructions, they will give them a pizza massage. Firstly, roll out the dough (roll fists over their back). Secondly, spread out the tomato paste (rub hands on their back). Next, cut up the ham, pineapple, salami, etc. (chop with the side of your hand) and place on individually a set number of pieces (12 pieces of ham, 6 pieces of pinapple etc.), counting them out. Then grate the cheese (use fingers to scratch) and sprinkle each ingredient on (use fingertips to sprinkle). Finally, warm up the pizza in the oven (rub their back fast), cut the pizza into 8 slices (slice with side of hand) and eat the pizza (grab at their back).

Magic Piece of Paper

To get the students to clean the room, tell them you have found a magic piece of paper. The person that picks it up will be revealed once the room is clean and will receive a sticker.

Minute Mime (page 133)

Give students an action to act out silently and the class will guess what they are.

Letter/Number Blind Draw

Draw letters or numbers on a partner's back and they have to guess what it is.

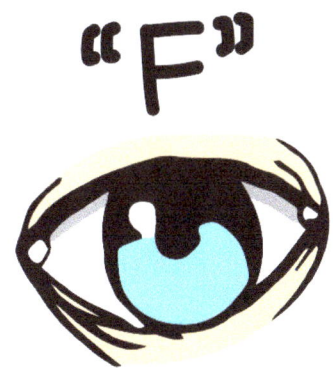

Eye Spy

Eye spy with my little eye, something beginning with… F. This old favourite is great to reinforce students' letter sound knowledge.

UPPER PRIMARY

Celebrity Heads

Three people at the front of the class are given a celebrity name to guess, and this is written behind their head. They can only ask 'yes' or 'no' questions for the class to answer.

Dots and Boxes

Students draw a 10 x 10 dot square and take turns to draw one line between the dots. When they make a square, they put their initial in it. The person with the most squares at the end of the game, wins.

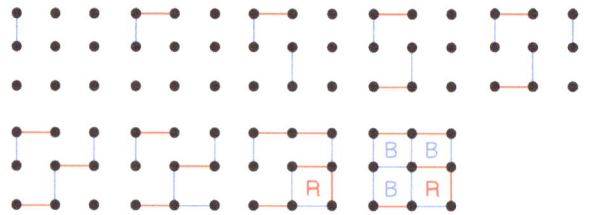

Silent Ball

Students stand silently and throw a ball to each other. If they talk, drop the ball or do a bad pass they have to sit down.
The winner is last person standing. You can add in actions such as stand on one foot, keep your hand behind your back etc.

Last Letter Game

Using a topic (can use examples in Scattegories), students in a circle will say a word then the next student needs to use the last letter of the word to choose their next word. E.g., Boys Names - Ben, Noah, Harrison, Neil, Luke etc. Animals - Dog, Goat, Tiger, Rabbit, Turtle, etc.

Scattegories

On the board, write down 10-15 different topics. On a piece of paper, students write down the numbers 1-10 or 15 and have 1 minute to answer each topic according to a certain letter that is called out. Topics could include boys/girls name, food, animal, vehicle, sport, actor, dessert, country, gift, job, TV show, singer, fruit, vegetable, city, song, drink, etc. Students call out answers but only get a point if no one else has that answer.

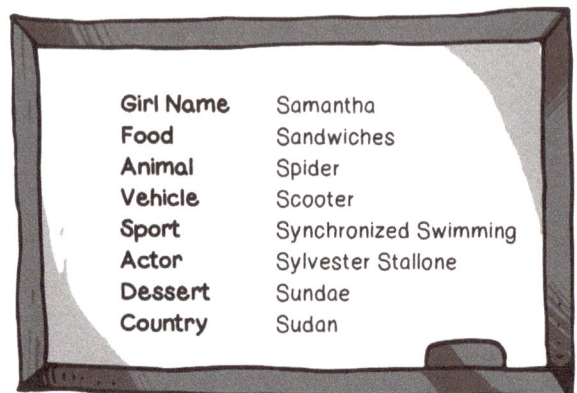

Girl Name	Samantha
Food	Sandwiches
Animal	Spider
Vehicle	Scooter
Sport	Synchronized Swimming
Actor	Sylvester Stallone
Dessert	Sundae
Country	Sudan

GAMES

148

Topic Talk

Students talk on a given or chosen topic for 1 minute trying not to say "um". Keep tally of how many "ums" are said and the winner is the student with the least "ums". Suggested topics- Friends, should students have homework, recycling, should we have a 3-day weekend, bananas etc.

Charades

Students act out a movie, TV show or book, breaking up the title into words and act out each word without speaking.

20 Questions

Choose a person, place or thing for the person to guess. The guesser can then ask up to 20 yes and no questions to try and work out the answer.

5 in 10

Divide the class into teams and each team (or the teacher) can decide on a topic. Students then need to give 5 answers in 10 seconds. Topics could extend on from what you are learning "Name 5 adverbs" or "Name 5 capital cities" or they can be random topics such as "Name 5 girl names that start with N" or "Name 5 types of dessert".

149

GAMES

LOWER PRIMARY and UPPER PRIMARY

Mr Squiggle

One student is chosen to be the judge and stands outside the door. The teacher draws a simple picture (e.g., circle, cross, wavy line) 3 times on the board. Three children are chosen to draw and they must create a picture using the squiggle.
The audience are the timekeepers and need to watch the clock for when 1 minute is up. The three children return to their desks, remaining anonymous so the judge can show no bias. The judge comes back and rubs off the two drawings he likes least, leaving his favourite on the board. The winner becomes the next judge.

Heads Down, Thumbs Up

4 or 5 students are chosen to stand up at the front of the class. The students at their desks close their eyes, put their heads down on the desk with their thumbs poking up beside their ears. The chosen students pick a child each by pushing their thumbs down and then return to the front of the class. The chosen students stand up and guesses who chose them. If they guess correctly they get to swap places with the person who chose them and have a turn at the front of the class.

Hang Ten

An alternative version to the original Hangman drawing a surfer on a board instead.

Pictionary

Split the class in half. Choose one student from each team to draw. Whisper a word to them both, then they have 30 seconds - 1minute to draw it. The first team to guess correctly gets a point.

Guess 1 minute

Get students to put their head down on the desk and raise it when 1 minute is up. The closest to the 60 second mark wins. Play it again if time permits and discuss why they didn't guess correctly.

Count to Twenty

The class needs to count to twenty by taking turns. Only one person can say a number at a time. If two or more people says a number together then they have to start counting again. Lower the number to 10 or 5 if they are finding it too difficult.

Grandma's Undies
(or socks if undies is too risqué!)

Sit in a circle or at desks, choose an "answerer" and the students need to ask them a question. The "answerer" must reply with "Grandma's undies." The catch is they cannot laugh or answer with anything other than "Grandma's undies" or they are out. Great to practice questioning.

Ask questions like -
- "What did you wear to bed last night?"
- "What do you think would scare away your Dad?"
- "What did you find in your desk this morning?"
- "What is the thing you love the most?"
- "What do you like to wear to school?"
- "What do you and your friends play with?"
- "What do you wash your face with?"
- "What would you give someone on Valentine's Day?"
- "What are you wearing on your head?"

Minute Mime

Whisper to a student a direction for them to act out silently. The person that guesses right gets to be the next mime. Refer to page 133 for ideas.

Voice Changer

One person is "it" and is blindfolded or closes their eyes. The teacher then chooses a student to say a phrase in a silly voice and the blindfolded student needs to guess who said it.

The Never Ending Sentence

Students say one word at a time and continue a sentence using connectives (and, like, but, then etc.)

GAMES

Around the World

One student stands behind another student who is sitting at their desk. The teacher asks them a question relevant to the subject and the first student to answer correctly moves on to the next desk.

Higher or Lower

Tell students you are thinking of a number between 1 and 100. Students guess numbers and you tell them whether the number you are thinking of is higher or lower, until they guess correctly.

Who is Missing

One person leaves the room. Another student is told to hide and when the student returns, this person must work out who is missing. This game works best when students are sitting in a circle or can change seats.

NOTES

You can teach a student a lesson for a day;
but if you can teach him to learn by creating curiosity, he
will continue the learning process as long as he lives.

-Clay P. Bedford

PE/Outdoor Games

LOWER PRIMARY and UPPER PRIMARY

Human Under & Over

Set students up as obstacles. One child in a ball, as a bridge, with legs spread out wide, etc. Students must jump over, under, through, around, etc. then run back to the start

Races

Divide students into equal teams and arrange them opposite each other, like a relay race. Students run to their other team and tag the next person. Use actions such as running, hopping, crawling, frog jumping, side stepping, grape-vining, running backwards, etc.

BBB Ball (Bounce Ball Behind)

Using a bouncy ball/basketball/netball, students must allow the ball to bounce once in front of them before pushing the ball backwards over their head. If the ball bounces twice and you are the closest to the ball you must sit out. If you throw the ball out on the full or the ball hits you on the full you are also out. The last person remaining, wins.

Stuck in the Mud/Toilet Game

You could play traditional stuck in the mud OR for a little fun, when students are tagged they must kneel down on one knee to be the toilet. Students must then squat over them and flush the toilet by pushing their hand down to set them free again.

Flush me!

Obstacle Course

Using a playground, trees, or basketball lines, give students an obstacle to complete. Jumping, climbing, weaving, crawling, running around in order.

Line Tiggy

Using a basketball court, students must walk/run only on the line while two students try to tag them. If you are tagged you must sit out until the next game.

Poison Letter

One person is the 'caller' at one end of a court/area while the rest of the class is at the other end. The caller identifies 2 poison letters, then proceeds to call out letters randomly. Students take a step for each letter called that they have in their name; 2 steps for capital letters. Anyone who steps when the poison letters are called out has to go back to the starting line. The first student to reach the caller is up next.

No Bat Baseball

Set up a small diamond using markers, jumpers etc. The class is split into two teams, batters and fielders. Using a large, bouncy ball, a pitcher will roll it to the 'batter' who will kick the ball to the fielders. The 'batter' must run around the whole diamond in order to get a point. If the fielders throw it back to the backstop before the batter runs home then they don't get a point. If 3 people or a whole team get out, the teams can switch place.

Dodge Ball

For an all-inclusive version of Dodge Ball, set up a square with cones. Choose 2-4 people to be the throwers who stand outside the square and everyone else is inside the square. The throwers have a ball each and must throw the ball and hit the players in the middle for them to get out. If a player is hit with the ball they then become a thrower to try and get more players out. If someone catches the ball on the full, they can choose someone else to come back in the middle to play again.

⬤ = ball   △ = cone

X = thrower   X = player

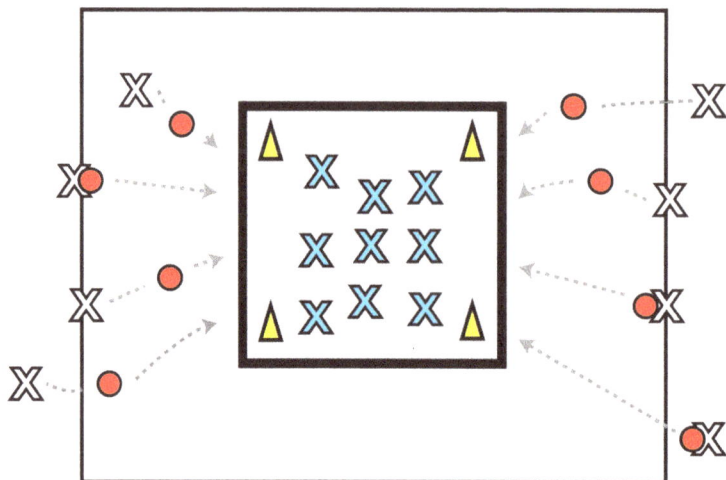

Capture the Flag

Split the class into two even teams and set the field up with cones to create four corners as pictured below. In two diagonal corners you will place a hula hoop and 4 flags/bean bags etc. inside each coned corner. In the other two diagonal corners you will set up a jail. Now the object of the game is to capture all the flags of your opposing team without getting tagged. If you get tagged you must go to their jail and can only leave if someone from your team saves you. You can only take one flag at a time and if you are tagged with a flag you must return the flag and go to jail. Get all 8 flags into your corner and your team wins. If the game goes too long, call time and the team with the most flags, wins.

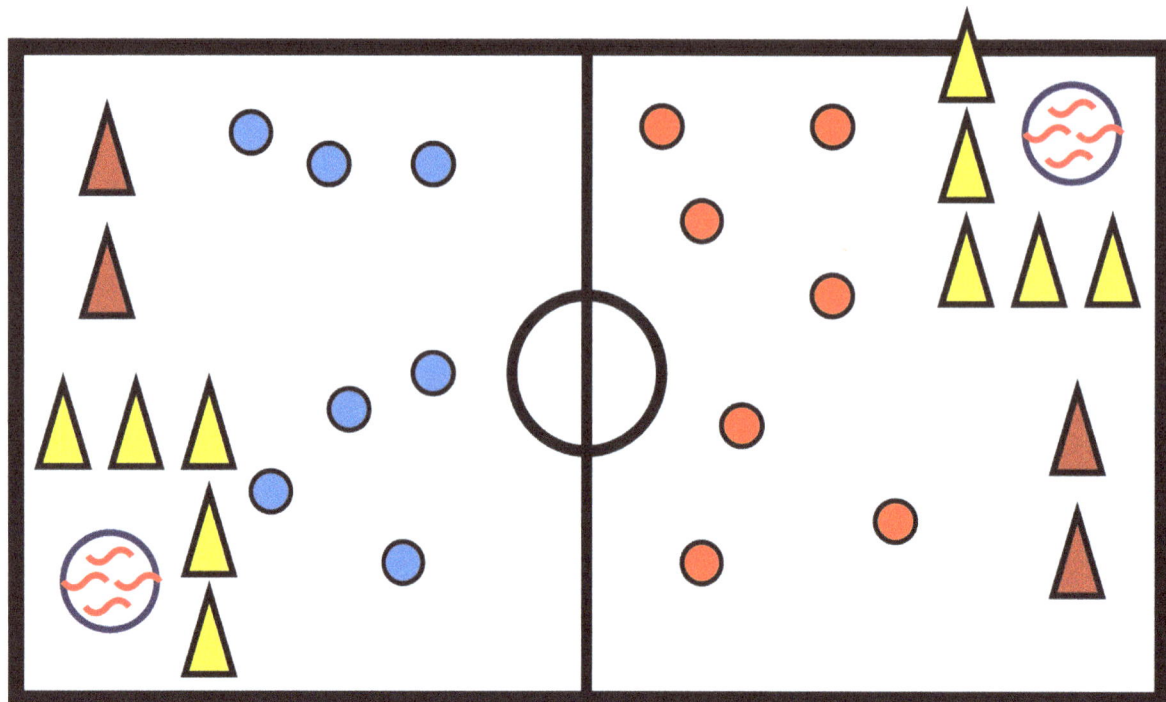

NOTES

www.ingramcontent.com/pod-product-compliance
Ingram Content Group UK Ltd.
Pitfield, Milton Keynes, MK11 3LW, UK
UKHW050309250925

8053UKWH00090B/1296

9 780995 405745